LANGUAGE BUILDER

In Sync 4

Rod Fricker
Ingrid Freebairn
Jonathan Bygrave
Judy Copage

Welcome to the **Language Builder!**

This **Language Builder** will give you more practice in the grammar, vocabulary, functions, and skills that are in your Student Book. The Language Builder is divided into two parts: a Workbook and a Grammar Bank.

Workbook

The first part of the Language Builder is the **Workbook**. This contains practice exercises for the grammar, vocabulary, functions, and skills in your Student Book. Most of the exercises in the Workbook lessons are at two levels of difficulty: easier (★) and more difficult (★★). There are also *Consolidation* exercises, which provide practice of several language points. In addition, there is an *Extra challenge!* exercise (★★★) in each unit, which gives you the opportunity to do a more challenging activity.

Grammar Bank

The second part of the Language Builder is the **Grammar Bank**. This contains *Grammar Summary* pages with examples and notes to help you remember grammar rules. These are followed by *Grammar Practice* exercises. You can do these exercises as a follow-up to the exercises in the Workbook, or you can use them later to help you review.

We hope that this Language Builder will help you in your English studies.

Have fun and stay *In Sync*!

Contents

Workbook				Grammar Bank
Unit	Page	Grammar	Vocabulary/Function	Grammar
1A	2	• Simple present and present continuous • Tag questions	• Clothes, styles, accessories, and patterns • Shop for clothes	**Page 99** • Simple present and present continuous • Tag questions • Present perfect and simple past • Present perfect with *for* or *since* • Intensifiers *much*, *a lot*, *a little* with comparative adjectives and adverbs; *(not) as . . . as*
1B	4	• Present perfect with *for* or *since*; simple past • Present perfect with *for* or *since*	• Jobs	
1C	6	• Intensifiers *much*, *a lot*, *a little* with comparative adjectives and adverbs; *(not) as . . . as*	• Adjectives to describe work	
1D	8	**Across cultures:** *Teenage fashion* **Integrated skills:** Consolidation **Learning strategy:** Collect and organize your ideas		
2A	10	• Simple past	• Show concern and reassure	**Page 103** • Simple past • Past continuous and simple past with *while* and *when* • Simple past and past perfect • *after/before* + gerund (-*ing* form)
2B	12	• Past continuous and simple past with *while* and *when*	• Phrasal verbs with *up*	
2C	14	• Simple past and past perfect • *after/before* + gerund (-*ing* form)	• Transportation and travel	
2D	16	**Curriculum link:** *History – Milestones in travel and transportation* **Integrated skills:** Consolidation **Learning strategy:** Dictionary skills (1)		
3A	18	• Future tenses: *will*, *be going to*, present continuous form • *be about to* + infinitive	• Food and kitchen equipment	**Page 106** • Future tenses: *will*, *be going to*, present continuous form • *be about to* + infinitive • Gerund (-*ing* form) as subject • *must*, *need*, *should*, *ought to*, *have to*, *had better* • *make*, *let*, *allowed to*
3B	20	• Gerund (-*ing* form) as subject • *must*, *need*, *should*, *ought to*, *have to*, *had better*	• Part-time jobs	
3C	22	• *make*, *let*, *allowed to*	• Invite, accept, and refuse with excuses	
3D	24	**Values for living:** *A refugee's story* **Integrated skills:** Consolidation		
4A	26	• Present perfect with *already*, *before*, *never*, *ever*, *yet* • Superlatives with the present perfect	• React to good and bad news	**Page 110** • Present perfect with *already*, *before*, *never*, *ever*, *yet* • Superlatives with the present perfect • Present perfect and present perfect continuous with *for* and *since* • Present perfect for numbers and amounts • Restrictive and nonrestrictive relative clauses
4B	28	• Present perfect and present perfect continuous with *for* and *since* • Present perfect for numbers and amounts	• Music words	
4C	30	• Restrictive and nonrestrictive relative clauses	• Phrasal verbs with *on*	
4D	32	**Across cultures:** *English literature* **Integrated skills:** Consolidation **Writing tip:** Conjunctions *as well as*, *what's more*, *not only . . . but also*		
5A	34	• Conditionals with *if*, *unless*, *provided that*, *as long as*	• Landforms and the environment	**Page 114** • Conditionals with *if*, *unless*, *provided that*, *as long as* • Future time clauses with *when*, *until*, *as soon as*, *by the time*, *before* • *in case* + simple present
5B	36	• Future time clauses with *when*, *until*, *as soon as*, *by the time*, *before*	• Extreme weather and natural disasters	
5C	38	• *in case* + simple present	• Camping equipment • Make and respond to requests	
5D	40	**Curriculum link:** *Geography – Glaciers* **Integrated skills:** Consolidation **Learning strategy:** Dictionary skills (2)		
6A	42	• Conditional: *if* clause + past	• Transitive phrasal verbs	**Page 117** • Conditional: *if* clause + past • *wish/if only* + simple past • Verb + infinitive or gerund
6B	44	• *wish/if only* + simple past	• Ask for and give advice	
6C	46	• Verb + infinitive or gerund	• Noun suffixes -*ion*, -*ment*, -*ity*, and -*y*	
6D	48	**Values for living:** *The prom* **Integrated skills:** Consolidation		

Contents

Workbook				Grammar Bank
Unit	Page	Grammar	Vocabulary/Function	Grammar
7A	50	• Reported statements and questions	• Phone messages	**Page 120** • Reported statements and questions • Reporting verbs • Subordinating conjunctions that show contrast
7B	52	• Reporting verbs		
7C	54	• Subordinating conjunctions that show contrast	• Relationship words and phrases	
7D	56	**Across cultures:** *Communication in the 21st century* **Integrated skills:** Consolidation **Writing tip:** *First, second,* and *last*		
8A	58	• *so* + adjective/adverb *(that)* . . ., *such a/an* + adjective + noun *(that)* . . ., *so many/much* + noun *(that)* . . ., Verb + *so much (that)* . . .	• Adjectives of emotion	**Page 124** • *so* + adjective/adverb *(that)* . . ., *such a/an* + adjective + noun *(that)* . . ., *so many/much* + noun *(that)* . . ., Verb + *so much (that)* . . . • *used to/be used to/get used to* • *be able to*
8B	60	• *used to/be used to/get used to*	• Ask for and give explanations	
8C	62	• *be able to*	• Phrasal verbs with *in*	
8D	64	**Curriculum link:** *Citizenship – Charity work* **Integrated skills:** Consolidation **Learning strategy:** Dictionary skills (3)		
9A	66	• Causative *have*	• Parts of a bike • Describe and deal with problems	**Page 128** • Causative *have* • Clauses of purpose: *to, in order (not) to, so that* • *look, seem, sound, feel, taste, smell* + adjective */like/as if*
9B	68	• Clauses of purpose: *to, in order (not) to, so that*	• Adjective suffixes with -*ful*, -*y*, -*ous*, -*ive*, -*al*	
9C	70	• *look, seem, sound, feel, taste, smell* + adjective */like/as if*	• Adjectives of texture and shape	
9D	72	**Values for living:** *Work experience* **Integrated skills:** Consolidation **Learning strategy:** Listen for linking phrases		
10A	74	• *should have/ought to have*	• Apologize for past mistakes	**Page 131** • *should have/ought to have* • *must/can't/might/could* for deductions in the present • *must have/can't have/might have/could have* for deductions in the past
10B	76	• *must/can't/might/could* for deductions in the present	• Phrasal verbs with *away*	
10C	78	• *must have/can't have/might have/could have* for deductions in the past	• Crime	
10D	80	**Across cultures:** *Social customs* **Integrated skills:** Consolidation **Writing tip:** *on the other hand, in spite of this, consequently, because of this*		
11A	82	• The passive: simple present, simple past, present perfect, past perfect	• The media	**Page 135** • The passive: simple present, simple past, present perfect, past perfect • The passive: present continuous, past continuous and simple future • The passive: modals, gerund (-*ing* form), and infinitive
11B	84	• The passive: present continuous, past continuous, and simple future	• Give opinions, agree, and disagree	
11C	86	• The passive: modals, gerund (-*ing* form), and infinitive	• Adjective and noun formation	
11D	88	**Curriculum link:** *Science – Nanotechnology* **Integrated skills:** Consolidation **Learning strategy:** Dictionary skills (4)		
12A	90	• Conditional: *if* clause + past perfect	• Verbs connected with money	**Page 139** • Conditional: *if* clause + past perfect • *wish/if only* + past perfect • Conditional: *if* clause + *might have*
12B	92	• *wish/if only* + past perfect	• Phrasal verbs with *out*	
12C	94	• Conditional: *if* clause + *might have*	• Give and accept congratulations	
12D	96	**Values for living:** *The inheritance* **Integrated skills:** Consolidation **Listening tip:** Use the task to guide you		

Lifestyles

1

Phrases

1 ★ Circle the correct answers.

Max: Excuse me, I'm looking for a present for my girlfriend.

Assistant: What are you **1** (looking for) / wanting?

Max: I'm not sure. **2** Something / Someone unusual. I want to surprise her.

Assistant: How about some silver bracelets?

Max: Oh, yeah, these are great. Oh no! There's my girlfriend now.

Laura: Hi, Max. How's it **3** doing / going?

Max: Laura! Hi! I thought you were home.

Laura: No. I meet Sue here **4** every / each other Saturday. We're going shopping today. I need some new clothes for my birthday party. **5** Anyway / Although, what do you have there?

Max: Oh . . . nothing, I have to go. See you later.

Vocabulary: Clothes, styles, accessories, and patterns

2a ★ Write the words.

1 b*andana*

2 s_____

3 s_____

4 h_____ _____

5 b_____

6 d_____

7 j_____

8 j_____

9 s_____

10 s_____

11 s_____

b ★ Match the adjectives (1–5) to the clothes (a–e).

1 high-heeled   a) pants

2 baggy   b) dress

3 striped   c) shoes

4 plain   d) shirt

5 checkered   e) sweater

Grammar: Simple present and present continuous

3 ★ Circle the correct form of the verbs.

FACESPACE GROUP

I love cool clothes!

Q: Where **1** (do you usually shop) / are you usually shopping for clothes?

2 I always buy / I'm always buying my clothes at the market. They **3** sell / are selling the coolest clothes.

Q: What **4** do you wear / are you wearing right now?

I'm at school right now. **5** I wear / I'm wearing a sweatshirt. The school is really cold today so **6** I don't wear / I'm not wearing cool clothes!

Q: Boys: **7** Do you ever wear / Are you ever wearing bracelets or **8** do you think / are you thinking they are only for girls?

Well, **9** I wear / I'm wearing some now. I wouldn't buy them but sometimes I **10** I borrow / I'm borrowing my sister's!

Grammar: Tag questions

4 ★ Match the beginnings (1–4) with the tag questions (a–d).

1 That's the new boy,   a) does he?

2 He's from Scotland,   b) isn't it?

3 He doesn't have his school   c) isn't he?
  uniform yet,   d) doesn't he?

4 He looks cool,

5 ★★ Complete the conversation with the correct tag questions.

Carlos: Hi. You're new here, **1** _aren't you_?
          I'm Carlos and this is Chrissie.

Ewan: Hi. Yes, I'm Ewan. It's a big school,
          2 _____? I'm a little nervous.

Carlos: Don't worry. We'll help you. We're nice,
          3 _____, Chrissie?

Chrissie: Yes, that's right. Do you know where you're
          going? You have a schedule, **4** _____?

Ewan: Yes, here it is. It's kind of confusing. Class
          starts in five minutes, **5** _____?

Chrissie: That's right and you're in room seventeen
          with Mr. King. That's this way. Come on.

Carlos: That's a cool T-shirt. Rihanna's a great
          singer, **6** _____?

Ewan: Yes, she's my favorite. I listen to her songs all
          the time. I have some on my phone here . . .

Carlos: You don't have a phone at school,
          7 _____? Quick, put it away! It's a
          school rule. No phones.

Ewan: Oh, right, thanks. I'm sure there are lots of
          things I need to know about this school.

Carlos: Yes. The first thing is that Mr. King hates
          people being late, **8** _____, Chrissie?

Use your English: Shop for clothes

6 ★ Put the conversations in the correct order.

Conversation 1

a) **Beth:**   Yes, please. I'm looking   ☐
                     for a shirt.

b) **Beth:**   It looks good. How much is it?   ☐

c) **Salesperson:** Can I help you?   1

d) **Beth:**   That's too expensive. Thanks   ☐
                     anyway.

e) **Salesperson:** How about this one?   ☐

f) **Salesperson:** It's $50.   ☐

Conversation 2

a) **Tim:**   Can I try the black ones on?   ☐

b) **Tim:**   Do you have these pants   ☐
                     in a different color?

c) **Salesperson:** Of course, the fitting   ☐
                     rooms are over there.

d) **Salesperson:** Yes, they come in black, red,   ☐
                     or brown.

Consolidation

7 Complete the sentences with the correct form of *do*, *be,* or *have*.

1 We _are_n't playing well today, _are_ we?

2 Where _____ you live?

3 You like soccer, _____ you?

4 Who _____ Pia talking to on the phone?

5 What _____ you have in your bag?

6 Your mom _____n't speak French,
  _____ she?

7 Stella and Alex _____n 't have a dog, _____
  they?

He's broken 24 bones.

Vocabulary: Jobs

1 ★ Find nine more jobs in the wordsearch.

X	H	O	M	E	M	A	K	E	R
P	P	N	U	R	S	E	C	N	B
B	I	A	M	T	Y	T	U	G	M
U	L	M	E	C	H	A	N	I	C
I	O	G	Q	T	K	I	R	N	A
L	T	R	C	A	S	H	I	E	R
D	E	T	E	C	T	I	V	E	T
E	W	M	V	X	Y	O	L	R	I
R	F	Y	K	O	P	I	W	M	S
J	O	U	R	N	A	L	I	S	T

Grammar: Present perfect with *for* or *since*; Simple past

2 ★ Read the article and circle the correct answers.

Barack Obama ¹ *was* / *has been* born in Hawaii in 1961. He ² *lived* / *has lived* there for six years and then his family ³ *moved* / *has moved* to Indonesia. He ⁴ *returned* / *has returned* to the U.S. at the age of ten and ⁵ *lived* / *has lived* there since then. In November 2008, he ⁶ *won* / *has won* the U.S. Presidential election. He ⁷ *was* / *has been* the president officially since January 20, 2009.

3 ★★ Read the interview. Complete the questions and answers with the verbs in the present perfect or the simple past.

1 Q: When *did* you *become* (become) President?
   A: I *became* (become) President on January 20, 2009.
2 Q: Where _____ your mom and dad _____ (meet)?
   A: They _____ (meet) in Hawaii, but my dad _____ (come) from Kenya.
3 Q: When _____ you _____ (get) your first job in politics?
   A: Well, I _____ (work) in local politics a long time ago when I lived in Chicago. I _____ (work) in national politics since 1996.
4 Q: How _____ you _____ (meet) your wife Michelle?
   A: We _____ (meet) in Chicago at work. We _____ (know) each other since 1989.
5 Q: _____ you _____ (write) any books?
   A: Yes, I _____ (write) two, so far. I _____ (write) *Dreams From My Father* in 1995 and *The Audacity of Hope* in 2008.
6 Q: _____ you _____ (see) the YouTube video of your "Yes, we can" speech with music?
   A: Yes, of course. I _____ (see) it a few times.

Grammar: Present perfect with *for* or *since*

4 ★ Put the verbs in parentheses in the correct form and then complete the sentences with *for* or *since*.

1 I *'ve been* (be) here ___*for*___ half an hour.
2 Our mom and dad _____ (be) married _____ 20 years!
3 Mr. Burns _____ (work) in our school _____ September.
4 Charles _____ (have) his MP3 player _____ last Tuesday.

Consolidation

5 Complete the ads. Use the pictures and the correct form of the verbs in the box.

• for • have • leave • not pass • since
• watch • not work • work

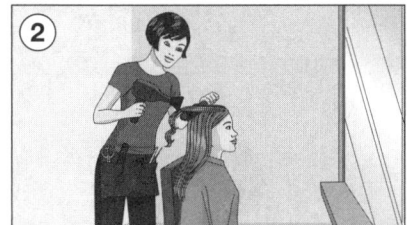

Job wanted:

I want to be a ¹ be*autician* . I ª _____ three jobs ᵇ _____ I left school in 2007. At the moment, I'm a ² h_____ . I work in Toni's Salon. I ᶜ _____ there ᵈ _____ six months. I like my job but now I want to learn something new.

Job wanted:

Do you need a ³ c_____ ? I ᵉ _____ school in 2003. I ᶠ _____ any classes at school and I ᵍ _____ for five years. I ʰ _____ lots of cooking shows on TV. It looks easy! I'm sure I would be good in a kitchen.

Extra challenge

6 ★★★ Complete the sentences with the verbs in the present perfect or the simple past. Then guess the correct answers and circle them.

Sean Connery

1 He *has been* (be) an actor since *1944 / 1954 / 1964*.
2 Before he became an actor, he _____ (be) a milkman, a body builder, and a *truck / taxi / train* driver.

Shontelle

3 In college, she _____ (study) to become a *doctor / teacher / lawyer*.
4 She _____ (know) *Beyonce / Rhianna / Halle Berry* since they were at school together.

Nicole Kidman

5 She _____ (work) for *UNICEF / NATO / UNESCO* since 1994.
6 She _____ (sing) "Something Stupid" with *George Michael / Sting / Robbie Williams*.

Gianfranco Zola

7 When he was a soccer player, he _____ (play) in Italy and *England / Spain / France*.
8 He _____ (be) a manager since *2004 / 2005 / 2006*.

Answers: 2 truck driver 3 lawyer 4 Rhianna 5 UNICEF 6 Robbie Williams 7 England 8 2006

Vocabulary: Adjectives to describe work

1 ★ Complete the adjectives to describe the jobs.

1 b _o_ _r_ _i_ _n_ g, b _ _ _ l _ p _ _ _ d

2 d _ _ g _ r _ _ _ _ , e _ c _ _ _ _ n _

3 g _ _ m _ _ o _ _ , w _ _ _ -p _ _ _ _

4 w _ _ t _ w _ _ _ _ _ , r _ w _ _ d _ _ _ _

2 ★★ Circle the correct answers.

This is a great opportunity. It's very ¹(creative)/ dull / stressful–use your artistic skills to make each burger different! The job can be very ² educational / exciting / tiring when a celebrity comes in for a burger. The uniform is very ³ glamorous / rewarding / worthwhile and the job is also ⁴ dangerous / well-paid / educational because you learn exactly how many fries are in a serving.

It's a ⁵ stressful / badly paid / interesting job–only $4.50 an hour! The work is ⁶ exciting / glamorous / boring–the same thing all day, every day. It's also ⁷ tiring / safe / educational because you are on your feet all day. It can be ⁸ rewarding / creative / dangerous, too–three people burned themselves last week!

Grammar: Intensifiers *much*, *a lot*, *a little* with comparative adjectives and adverbs; *(not) as . . . as*

3 ★ Circle the correct answers.

1 Teachers aren't as badly paid (as)/ *than* / *like* nurses.

2 House cleaners work *more hard* / *harder* / *more hardly* than salespeople.

3 You should think about your work *careful* / *more careful* / *more carefully*.

4 Please drive *slower* / *more slow* / *more slowly*!

5 My new job is *easier* / *more easy* / *more easily* than my old one, but it isn't as *good-* /*well-* / *better-* paid.

6 I earn *fewer* / *worse* / *less* than you, and I work *a lot* / *as* / *much* longer than you each day.

7 Why aren't you as *happy* / *happily* / *more happy* as I am?

8 I'm getting *a little* / *better* / *a lot* more money than last year, but not much.

4 ★★ Compare the activities using the information given.

| ✓✓ | much more | = | as . . . as |
| ✓ | a little more | ✗ | not as . . . as |

Backpacking/Doing volunteer work

1 doing volunteer work ✓✓ backpacking (difficult)

Doing volunteer work is much more difficult than backpacking.

2 doing volunteer work ✓ backpacking (interesting)

_____

_____

3 backpacking ✗ doing volunteer work (dangerous)

_____

_____

4 backpacking = doing volunteer work (rewarding)

_____

_____

Working in a store/Being a waiter

5 being a waiter ✓✓ working in a store (tiring)

_____

_____

6 being a waiter ✓ working in a store (glamorous)

_____

_____

7 working in a store ✗ being a waiter (stressful)

_____

_____

8 working in a store = being a waiter (dull)

_____

_____

Consolidation

5 Complete each sentence so that it matches the one above it. Use the words in parentheses.

1a My new job is much better paid than my old one. (much/badly paid)

1b My old job was *much more badly paid than* my new one.

2a A rock star's life is much more exciting than a teacher's life. (a lot/dull)

2b A teacher's life is _____

_____ a rock star's life.

3a A police officer's job is a lot safer than a soldier's. (much/dangerous)

3b A soldier's job is _____

_____ a police officer's.

4a An artist is much more creative than a secretary. (as/creative)

4b A secretary is not _____

_____ an artist.

5a Working in a café is much more relaxing than working in a busy restaurant. (much/stressful)

5b Working in a busy restaurant is _____

_____ a café.

6a Taxi drivers drive more carefully than truck drivers. (as/careful)

6b Truck drivers don't drive _____

_____.

Across cultures

INTEGRATED CONSOLIDATION SKILLS

Teenage fashion

Read

1 ★ **Match the headings (1–5) to the correct quotes (A–E).**

1 A shopping mall ☐ 2 Other people ☐ 3 A market ☐ 4 Garage sales A 5 Thrift shops ☐

A My parents are members of a local theater group and they often organize these to raise money. I always help them because I often find something for myself when I sort out the donations. Of course I always pay for stuff but nothing costs more than $5!

B I rarely buy new clothes. These stores are great for finding unusual old jackets, pants, and shirts that people don't want anymore. They're really cheap and the money you spend all goes to people who need help.

C My friends and I usually take the bus here on Saturdays. It's great. There are 130 stores, four restaurants, and a movie theater. Some of the stores are expensive, but there are often sales so you can usually find some good bargains.

D This is a great place to buy clothes. I love walking around the different stalls. There's a roof so it doesn't matter if it's raining. The only problem is that there are no fitting rooms so, if you want to try things on, everyone can see you! It's OK for jackets and sweaters, but not pants.

E I don't like shopping and I don't follow fashion. I'm happy to wear whatever my parents buy for me. If I really want something special, I ask my parents or other relatives to buy it for me for my birthday. Last year my aunt bought me a great leather jacket. Well, she gave me the money and I bought it.

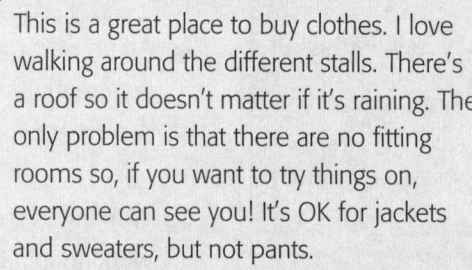

New words and phrases

2 ★★ Match the new words or phrases (1–4) with the definitions (a–d).

1 raise money   a) a large table in a public place where people sell things

2 sort out   b) to collect money for people or organizations

3 stall   c) times of the year when products are sold more cheaply than usual

4 sales   d) to organize or arrange things in a neat way

Comprehension

3 ★★ Read the quotes again and write *T* (true), *F* (false), or *DK* (don't know).

1 Quote A: The best thing about helping is that you don't have to pay for the clothes that you find.   *F*

2 Quote B: The clothes sold here are not new. ___

3 Quote C: The girl and her friend usually go to the movies after shopping. ___

4 Quote D: You can't try clothes on here because there are no fitting rooms. ___

5 Quote E: The leather jacket was a complete surprise for the boy. ___

Listen

4 ★ 2 Listen to a girl talking about some of the people in her class. Match each person to the clothes she mentions.

1 Matt   a) hats

2 Emma   b) bandanas

3 Sam   c) T-shirts

4 Jack   d) boots

5 Natalie   e) different clothes

5 ★★ Listen again and write where they buy their clothes.

1 Matt _____ *online* _____

2 Emma _____

3 Sam _____

4 Jack _____

5 Natalie _____

Write

Learning strategy: Collect and organize your ideas
Remember! Before you start to write, take time to collect and organize your ideas. First, make a list of all your ideas in any order. Then organize them into groups under headings.

6 ★ You are going to write an essay with the title "A friend whose fashion style I admire." Make notes of the information you want to include in your article.

Friend's name: _____

His or her clothes or accessories: _____

_____

_____

_____

_____

Extra information (where he or she buys his or her clothes; what influences his or her fashion taste, etc.):

_____

_____

_____

_____

7 ★★ Write the essay on a separate sheet of paper. Use your notes from Exercise 6 to help you.

A friend whose fashion style I admire
The friend I want to write about is . . .

I didn't recognize you.

Phrases

1 ★ Complete the conversations with phrases from the box.

> • I bet you're glad • I'd better get going • ~~No problem~~ • You'll get the hang of it

1 **Russ:** I'm sorry I'm late.

  Tim: _No problem_. No one else has arrived.

2 **Pete:** I'll never be able to play the guitar well.

  John: Don't worry. _____.
  Just keep practicing.

3 **Liz:** Beth said the movie was awful last night.

  Debbie: _____ you didn't go.

4 **Dave:** What time's your train?

  Ed: Nine o'clock. _____
  or I'll miss it.

Grammar: Simple past

2 ★ Complete the text with the simple past form of the verbs in parentheses.

Shaun White ¹ _was_ (be) born in 1986 in California. Doctors ² _____ (discover) a problem with his heart when he was five, but he ³ _____ (have) two successful operations. ⁴ He _____ (start) snowboarding when he was thirteen years old. It ⁵ _____ (not take) him long to win his first competition.

He ⁶ _____ (win) silver in the Winter X Medals competition in 2002, but then he ⁷ _____ (not win) another _silver_ medal until 2007. From 2003 to 2006, the only medals he ⁸ _____ (win) were gold! He also ⁹ _____ (go) to the Winter Olympics in Torino (2006) and Vancouver (2010). Each time he ¹⁰ _____ (return) home with another gold medal.

Shaun is now a multi-media star. There's a DVD about his Olympic success, a snowboarding documentary, and there was a joke about him in the movie _Ocean's 13_!

3 ★★ Complete the Internet chat with the correct form of the verbs in the box.

> • ask • come • forget • go • not be • not go
> • not watch • ~~see~~ • see • win

- Hi, Tim.
- Hello, Nick. ¹ _Did_ you _see_ the snowboarding finals last night?
- No, I didn't. I ² _____ all about it. ³ _____ Shaun White _____?
- No, he ⁴ _____ in second. I can't believe that you ⁵ _____ it. You love snowboarding.
- I know but, I ⁶ _____ home last night.
- Really? Where ⁷ _____ you _____?
- To the movies.
- What ⁸ _____ you _____?
- A romantic comedy.
- What? You hate romantic comedies.
- I know but I ⁹ _____ alone. I went with Melanie Stevens.
- No way! Tell me all about it. When ¹⁰ _____ you _____ her out?
- Well . . .

Grammar: Simple past

4 ★ Complete the conversation with the correct form of the verbs in parentheses.

http://www.facebook.com

Lisa: Hi Carlos. We ¹ *missed* (miss) you last weekend. What ² _____ (happen)?

Carlos: I ³ _____ (hurt) my shoulder windsurfing. I ⁴ _____ (spend) all day Saturday at the hospital!

Lisa: Oh, no! Are you OK now?

Carlos: Yes, but the doctor ⁵ _____ (give) me a cast, and I can't move my shoulder! Anyway, how was the party?

Lisa: It ⁶ _____ (be) really fun. Sophie ⁷ _____ (bring) her computer with all her music, so we ⁸ _____ (dance) a lot.

Carlos: ⁹ _____ Sergio ¹⁰ _____ (come)?

Lisa: Yes, he ¹¹ _____ (come), but he ¹² _____ (leave) early.

Carlos: Oh, well. Sounds like a fun party. Sorry I ¹³ _____ (miss) it.

Use your English: Show concern and reassure

5 ★ Circle the correct answers.

Conversation 1

Mom: What happened to you?

Jason: I **1** *fall /* (*fell*) */ feel* off my bike. A car went by really quickly and I lost my **2** *balance / weight / wheels*.

Mom: Did you **3** *hurt / pain / damage* yourself?

Jason: No, don't **4** *mind / hurry / worry*. I'm fine, but my bike isn't!

Conversation 2

Dad: Are you **5** *OK / right / good*?

Louise: Yes. I had an accident on my skateboard. My knee hurts a little, but it's nothing.

Dad: Can I **6** *do / help / find* anything?

Louise: No, I'm fine.

Dad: Are you **7** *real / sure / worry*?

Louise: Well, can you help me to the sofa?

Dad: OK. No **8** *surely / really / problem*.

Consolidation

6 Complete the conversation with words from the box. Put the verbs in the correct form.

> • bet • better • break • do • ~~during~~ • fall
> • for • hang • not do • not go • with

Will: Hi, Nicole. What did you do **1** *during* summer vacation?

Nicole: I was at a great summer camp **2** _____ two weeks. There was so much to do. My parents were in a quiet village in the country.

Will: I **3** _____ you're glad you **4** _____ with them. What activities **5** _____ you _____ at camp?

Nicole: I tried horseback riding. It was hard at first but I began to get the **6** _____ of it by the end. How was your vacation?

Will: Not very good. I **7** _____ anything.

Nicole: Why not?

Will: I broke my leg on the first day of the vacation.

Nicole: Oh no! How **8** _____ you _____ it?

Will: I **9** _____ down the stairs at home . . . don't laugh.

Nicole: Sorry. Come on, we'd **10** _____ get to school.

Vocabulary: Phrasal verbs with *up*

1 ★ Circle the correct verbs.

From: Cath
To: Mel

Hi, Mel,

I'm back. Summer camp was awful! Every day was the same: We had to ¹(wake)/ *stand* /*give* up at 6 A.M., then ² *hurry* / *get* / *take* up and clean the bedroom. We had to ³ *take* / *grow* / *pick* up all our clothes from the floor and then make our beds.

The food was terrible! We always had breakfast at 7:30, then we didn't eat again until we had lunch at 1 P.M. I was always hungry! And guess what! When the counselors came in to the dining hall, we all had to ⁴ *stand* / *get* / *pack* up until they sat down.

I'll tell you about the classes and activities when I see you. How was your vacation?

Cath

From: Mel
To: Cath

Hi Cath,

Sorry to hear about your nightmare camp! I had a great time. I really wanted to do something new, so I ⁵ *found* / *looked* / *picked* up some activities on the Internet. In the end, I ⁶ *worked* / *made* / *took* up tennis. I was worried that it would be very crowded but only five people ⁷ *took* / *came* / *showed* up on the first day. I had my own teacher every day. It was great! I went every day for two weeks and really enjoyed it. I'm going to be a tennis champion when I ⁸ *grow* / *come* / *get* up!

See you soon,

Mel

Grammar: Past continuous and simple past with *while* and *when*

2 ★ Complete the text with the past continuous or simple past form of the verbs in parentheses.

Stephen Bradbury was an Australian speed skater. In the 1994 Winter Olympics, he ¹ _was winning_ (win) when another skater ² _____ (push) him and he ³ _____ (fall). Later in the same year, he ⁴ _____ (race) in Montreal when another skater ⁵ _____ (hit) him and ⁶ _____ (cut) his leg.

In 2002, his luck changed. In the Winter Olympics final, he ⁷ _____ (be) in last place when the other four skaters all ⁸ _____ (crash) into each other. While they ⁹ _____ (lie) on the ice, Steven ¹⁰ _____ (skate) past them. He won the gold medal and became an Australian sports hero!

3 ★★ Write sentences with *while* or *when* and the past continuous or simple past. Do not change the order of the words.

1 Connor / break leg / play soccer

   Connor _broke his leg while he was playing soccer_.

2 Molly's phone / ring / take a test

   Molly's phone _____

   _____.

12

3 I / play a video game / computer crash

I _____

_____.

4 Will and Dave / walk in the park / see a rare bird

Will and Dave _____

_____.

5 Charlotte / meet some cool people / hike in France

Charlotte _____

_____.

4 ★★ Use the cues to complete the conversations. Use the past continuous or simple past and add *while* or *when* if necessary.

Paula: Hi, Beth. We had a normal day at school today but Mr. Smith was really angry with us.

Beth: Why?

Paula: **1** We / not sit / quietly / he / come in

We weren't sitting quietly when he came in.

Beth: **2** What / you / do / ?

_____

Paula: **3** I / read / a book

_____

but other people weren't so quiet.

Beth: **4** Tom and Mike / fight / ?

_____

Paula: Yes, they were. As usual!

5 Mr. Smith / come / in, some people / not hear / him

_____

The room slowly got quieter as people noticed him. Nick was looking out the window. He was the last one to notice Mr. Smith.

6 He turn / around, everyone else / sit / at their desks.

_____

_____

Beth: **7** What / he / do?

_____

Paula: He turned bright red and sat down!

Consolidation

5 Complete the text with the correct form of the words in the box.

• go • grow • look • make • see • show
• ~~take~~ • wake • when • while

Your questions asked.
This week, the actor Eric Galarza.

So, Eric, welcome to *Meet the Stars*. You're here today to answer a few questions about your life as an actor.

Why did you [1] __*take*__ **up acting?**
Well, [2] _____ I left high school, I [3] _____ to college in Mexico City. One day, [4] _____ I was walking to a class, I [5] _____ an ad for the theater drama group. I went to the next meeting and, amazingly, I discovered that I was good at acting and I enjoyed it.

Where did you [6] _____ **up?**
In a small, boring town called Littlefun about two hours from Mexico City. I lived there until I went to college.

Why didn't you [7] _____ **up at the Oscars last year?**
Ah, well. When I heard that one of my movies might win, I [8] _____ a movie in Vietnam. I had to stay there until everything was finished. I [9] _____ up flights on the Internet, and I booked a ticket from Vietnam to Los Angeles. We finally finished filming the night before my flight. There was a party to celebrate and I didn't get to bed until 6 A.M.! The hotel receptionist forgot to [10] _____ me up, and I missed my flight!

Grammar: Simple past and past perfect

1 ★ Look at the pictures and complete the sentences.

When Bob arrived at the station, the train *had left* (leave).

By the time Mark turned up at the party, all the food _____ (go).

When Paula opened her school bag, she realized that she _____ (leave) her books at home.

The car crashed into the tree because the driver _____ (fall) asleep.

Phil _____ (forget) to turn off his cell phone before the movie started.

2 ★★ Complete the text with the simple past or the past perfect form of the verbs in the box.

> • ask • book • catch • come • fly • get
> • happen • make • take

When Samantha booked her vacation from Spain to Costa Rica she didn't expect to arrive in Puerto Rico! When she asked a taxi driver at the airport to take her to her hotel in San José, he laughed. He told her that she **1** *had come* to the wrong country. What **2** _____ ? Samantha's travel agent **3** _____ a mistake. Samantha **4** _____ for a ticket to San José, the capital of Costa Rica. However, the travel agent **5** _____ her a ticket to San Juan, the capital of Puerto Rico!

There were no flights from Puerto Rico to Costa Rica. First, Samantha **6** _____ to Miami in the U.S. Then she **7** _____ a plane to San José. The journey from San Juan to San José **8** _____ four days.

Now everyone is asking the same question. How **9** _____ she _____ on the plane without realizing that it was going to the wrong country?

Grammar: *after/before* + gerund (*-ing* form)

3 ★ Look at the notes and complete the sentences on page 15.

Our tour of Europe
1 get off plane - take taxi to central London
2 check into hotel - go on the London Eye
3 take the train to Paris - buy some French bread - climb the Eiffel Tower
4 arrive in Rome - visit the Coliseum
5 walk around Pompeii - fly to Greece
6 land in Athens - take a boat to an island
7 spend two days on the beach - fly home

1   <u>*After getting off the plane*</u>, we took a taxi
to central London.

2 *Before going on the London Eye*, we checked
into our hotel.

3 _____,
we bought some French bread.

4 _____,
we visited the Coliseum.

5 _____,
we flew to Greece.

6 _____,
we took a boat to an island.

7 _____,
we spent two days on the beach.

Vocabulary: Transportation and travel

4 ★ Circle the correct answers.

Dear Parent/Caregiver,

School trip to Seattle, June 14

On Friday, we are planning to ¹ *miss /* (*catch*) the early
train. Please make sure your child is at the station by
8:10 A.M. We will ² *arrive / reach* in Seattle at 11 A.M.
After getting ³ *off / out* the train, we will go straight to
the Science Museum. If your child ⁴ *misses / changes*
the train, we can't wait for him or her in Seattle.

Dear Rachel,
I'm in pain in Spain! My mom and dad don't realize
how tall I am. We got a car from the airport. I
couldn't get ⁵ *on / in* or ⁶ *out / off* and I had
to sit in the back. By the time we ⁷ *reached /
arrived* our hotel, my back and legs really hurt.

To:	Stacy Kim, Manager
From:	Li Po Woo

I have to go to Beijing next week. Please, can I
travel by train this time? I hate flying. I hate it
when the plane ⁸ *takes / gets* off and I hate it
when it ⁹ *reaches / lands*. The worst thing about
flying to Beijing is that I have to ¹⁰ *change /
leave* planes in Seoul and do everything twice!

Consolidation

5 Complete the sentences with the correct
form of the verbs in parentheses. Then put the
sentences in the correct order to write a postcard.

Dear Steve,
We're finally here on vacation but we had a difficult trip.
We decided to get a taxi to the train station.

a) By the time the plane took off, we <u>*had spent*</u> (spend) half
of our vacation money! ☐

b) After _____ (call) the taxi, we waited outside
the house. [1]

c) After _____ (land) in Portland, we waited for
our bags. We waited and waited. ☐

d) After _____ (go) to our hotel, we had to spend
more money on clothes because we had nothing else to wear. ☐

e) We called a second taxi. When we arrived at the train
station, our train _____ (already/leave). ☐

f) Finally, we found out that our bags _____ (go)
to Portland, Maine by mistake. ☐

g) We couldn't get in the first taxi because we
_____ (take) so many bags. ☐

h) We got the next train and went to the airport. Before
_____ (get) on the plane, Mom and Dad
bought loads of presents. ☐

I hope the rest of the vacation is better than the start.
See you soon,
Natalie

Extra challenge

6 ★★★ Complete the sentences so that they
are true for you.

1 After getting home from school yesterday, I _____
_____.

2 After _____
last Saturday, I watched TV.

3 Before _____
last Friday, I did my homework.

4 Before the start of this year, I had never _____
_____.

5 By the time I was ten years old, I had _____
_____.

INTEGRATED
CONSOLIDATION
SKILLS

Milestones in travel and transportation

A

B

C

Read

1 ★ Read the postcards (1–3) and match the photos (A–C) with the correct postcards.

1 ☐ B

Dear Chris,
We're in Paris. It's a beautiful city. The trip only took two hours. We traveled on the high-speed Eurostar train. It travels at almost 190mph! I was scared about going under the ocean but it was fine. It was so quick! I was reading a pamphlet about the tunnel on the train and, when I looked up, we were in France! The first person to think of the idea of a channel tunnel was Napoleon in 1802. We're going to see Napoleon's tomb at Les Invalides here in Paris later!
See you soon, Jess

2 ☐

Dear Aunt Eileen,
We're in Italy. Yesterday, we were in Chamonix in France and this morning we drove through the tunnel under Mont Blanc. It was amazing. It's about seven miles long and goes from Chamonix in France to Courmayeur in Italy. It took eight years to build it. Now we're in Aosta. There are lots of Roman remains here, and we had a real Italian pizza for lunch! Tomorrow we're going to Verona. Then, no more driving for a week! Hooray! See you soon.
Love, Mel

3 ☐

Dear Grandma and Grandpa,
We're in Copenhagen in Denmark. It's a beautiful city. We flew to Malmo with a budget airline but the best part of the trip was the train ride from Malmo to Copenhagen on the Oresund bridge–tunnel. It's fantastic. From Malmo, it's a bridge. It's 187 feet above the sea. Then, in the middle of the sea, there's an island called Peberholm and the bridge turns into a tunnel.
We're going sightseeing today but the bridge is the best.
Love, Danny

Learning strategy: Dictionary skills (1)
Remember! If you need to use a dictionary, use a good American-English dictionary. When you look up the meaning of a new word, you will also see how to pronounce the word and what part of speech it is.

New words and phrases

2 ★★ Look up the new words in a dictionary. Circle the correct answers.

1 a) *pamphlet* is a (i) noun) ii) adjective iii) verb

   b) *pamphlet* means

   [i) a small book with a paper cover with information inside it]

   ii) a large magazine with articles and photographs

2 a) *tomb* is pronounced   i) /tɒm/   ii) /tum/

   b) *tomb* means

   i) a place where someone's body is kept after they have died

   ii) a house where a famous person spent most of their lives

3 *remains*

   a) is a   i) noun   ii) adjective   iii) verb

   b) is pronounced   i) /rɪˈmeɪnz/   ii) /rɪˈmeɪns/

   c) are

   i) shops selling Roman clothes and souvenirs

   ii) objects left from Roman times

4 a) *budget* (airline) is pronounced

      i) /bʌdʒɪt/   ii) /bʌdʒit/

   b) A budget airline company is

      i) cheap   ii) high quality

3 ★★ **Read the text again and explain the numbers and places.**

1 190mph *The Eurostar train travels at almost* _____

   190 miles per hour. _____

2 France to Italy _____

   _____

3 Peberholm _____

   _____

Listen

4 ★ 🎧 3 **Listen to a teacher and her students and name the two boats. Use the words below.**

| • SARK • MOTH • GIPSY • CUTTY |

1 _____   2 _____

5 ★★ **Listen again and complete the information about the two boats.**

1 The *Gipsy Moth* is _____ feet long.
   Sir Francis Chichester sailed around the world in it.

2 He left on August _____, 19 _____.

3 After 107 days, he stopped in _____, Australia.

4 He returned to England after sailing for _____ days.

5 The *Cutty Sark* is about _____ years old.

6 It is a "clipper." Clippers were very _____ boats.

7 The *Cutty Sark* sailed from England to China to bring back _____.

8 It also brought back wool from _____.

Write

6 ★★ **On a separate sheet of paper, write a three-paragraph biography about Sir Francis Chichester. Use the dates below, the information you heard in Exercise 5, and the Writing bank on page 144 of the Student Book to help you. Write a paragraph on his life before the journey, his life during the journey, and his life after the journey.**

1901	Born: Barnstable, Devon
1918	Moved to New Zealand
1929	Left New Zealand
1930s	Was a pilot and flew a plane called *Gipsy Moth*
1960	Won the first single-handed yacht race across the Atlantic
1966	Set off on his journey round the world (8/27/66) Journey: Plymouth, England – Australia (around the bottom of Africa). 48 days rest. Australia – England (around the bottom of South America)
1967	Arrived back (5/28/67)
1967	Became Sir Francis Chichester
↓	Continued sailing
1970	Sailed 4,000 miles in 20 days
1972	Died

Responsibility

3

Vocabulary: Food and kitchen equipment

1 ★ Look at the pictures and complete the chart.

Dishes	Silverware	Cooking utensils
		1 *sieve*

Grammar: Future tenses: *will*, *be going to*, present continuous form

2 ★ Circle the correct answers.

Annie: Hi, Olivia. Where are you going?

Olivia: I'm going shopping. I have $30 and
1 (*I'm going to buy*) / *I'll buy* some CDs.
What about you?

Annie: 2 *I'll meet* / *I'm meeting* Kate at the market.
3 *We'll go* / *We're going* to a party next
Saturday so 4 *we're going to look for* /
we'll look for some cool new T-shirts. Why
don't you come with us?

Olivia: No, it's OK. 5 *I'm not going to stay* / *I won't
stay* in town long. My dad's boss and his wife
6 *will come* / *are coming* for dinner. I'm sure
my mom 7 *will be* / *is being* nervous so I'm
8 *helping* / *going to help* her cook.

3 ★★ Complete each conversation with the
correct form of the words from the box. Use
will, *be going to*, and the present continuous in
each conversation.

1 | • have   • help   • make |

Emily: What are you doing this afternoon, Dad?

Dad: I*'m going to make* a cake.

Emily: Why?

Dad: Did you forget? It's your mom's birthday
tomorrow and we*'re having* a party.

Emily: Oh, yes! I*'ll help* you if you like.

Dad: Thanks. You can wash the cake pan.

2 | • play   • stop   • watch |

Ryan: I'm tired. I think I_____ working
for a while and rest.

Ben: I_____ the soccer game later.
Seattle _____ Los Angeles. Let's
watch it together.

3 | • be   • do   • leave |

Dad: We_____ on Saturday for our
vacation, and there's a lot to do before
then. It_____ a busy week.

Hannah: I_____ the laundry if you want,
and then I can pack the clothes.

4 | • meet   • spend   • not talk |

Mom: Juan, Dan wants to go to the movies, too.

Juan: Oh, Mom! I_____ my friends
there. Do I have to take him?

Mom: Don't be so mean. He _____ to you
or your friends. He just wants to see the movie.

Juan: But we want to do something afterwards.
We_____ the whole evening
together. How will Dan get home?

Mom: Don't worry. He can stay up late for once.

Grammar: *be about to* + infinitive

4 ★ **Match the beginnings (1–6) with the endings (a–f). Put the verbs in parentheses in the correct form and add *be about to*.**

1 I

2 My dad

3 My mom

4 My sister

5 My brother

6 My dog

a) _____ (open) a can of food.

b) _____ (wash) a dirty knife and fork.

c) *'m about to boil* _____ (boil) some water in the kettle.

d) _____ (eat) out of his bowl.

e) _____ (peel) a potato.

f) _____ (grate) some cheese.

Consolidation

5 **Complete the conversation with verbs from the box and write the words for the pictures.**

> • are going to take • I'll ask • I'll see • I'm going to bring • is about to fall • is bringing • ~~is going to bring~~

Group leader: Hi, everyone. Remember everyone

1 *is going to bring* something for the camp

which starts on Saturday. Has anyone

thought about what to bring?

Jack: Yes, I've decided. **2** _____

3 _____ and a

4 _____.

Natalie: My parents **5** _____ me to the

campsite by car so we can carry heavy

things like plates and

6 _____.

Group leader: Wonderful! Can they bring a

7 _____, too?

Natalie: **8** _____ them.

Group leader: Awesome. How about you Tim? Tim!

I think Tim **9** _____ asleep.

Natalie: I think he has fallen asleep. Tim, wake up!

Tim: What? Yes? um . . . sorry, I wasn't listening.

Group leader: I know. I said, can you bring anything

for the camp?

Tim: Um, yes, OK. I can bring some saucepans if

you like.

Group leader: No, Jack **10** _____ them.

What about some knives and

11 _____?

Tim: OK, **12** _____ what I can do.

Vocabulary: Part-time jobs

1 ★ Match the beginnings of the job ads (1–8) with the endings (a–h).

1 If you like animals, why not try dog

2 Two strong young people needed to mow

3 We need friendly, smart, young people to work in our

4 Local newspaper needs boys and girls for early morning newspaper

5 Have you thought about helping in

6 Help others by teaching

7 Volunteers needed to weed

8 Just moved into a new house? We'll do your painting and

a) lawns.

b) yards.

c) store.

d) decorating.

e) walking?

f) computer skills.

g) a retirement home?

h) deliveries.

Grammar: Gerund (-*ing* form) as subject

2 ★ Complete the sentences using the gerund (-*ing* form) of the verbs.

1 It isn't easy to teach English.

____Teaching____ English isn't easy.

2 It's tiring to take dogs for a walk.

_____ dogs for a walk is tiring.

3 It's boring to serve customers in a store.

_____ customers in a store is boring.

4 It's hard work to weed people's yards.

_____ people's yards is hard work.

5 It's great to earn money by working part time.

_____ money by working part time is great.

Grammar: *must, need, should, ought to, have to, had better*

3 ★ Look at the information about part-time jobs and complete the sentences with *should,* *shouldn't, have to,* or *don't have to.*

Part-time jobs—your opinions of the good, the bad, and the ugly!

Dog walking (Your rating ****)

Good things
1 No uniform
2 Not inside all day

Bad things
3 Early start
4 Cleaning up!

Advice
5 Make sure you're in good shape
6 No more than two dogs at one time!

1 You *don't have to wear* (wear) a uniform.

2 You _____ (work) inside.

3 You _____ (get up) early.

4 You _____ (clean up) when your dog makes a mess!

5 You _____ (be) in good shape.

6 You _____ (take) more than two dogs at one time.

4 ★★ Complete each sentence so that it matches the one above it. Use the words in parentheses.

Advice for delivering papers

1a It is necessary to get up early.

1b You ___*must get up*___ (must) early.

2a You'll need to buy a good bike.

2b You _____ (better) a good bike.

3a You can have your MP3 player on because there's no one to listen to or talk to.

3b You _____ (don't have to) or talk to anyone so you can have your MP3 player on.

4a My advice is to watch out for dogs in people's yards.

4b You _____ (ought to) for dogs in people's yards.

5a It's not a good idea to go to bed late.

5b You _____ (shouldn't) late.

6a You can wear your old clothes—no one expects you to dress up.

6b You _____ (don't have to).

7a Remember that even when it's raining you can't stay in bed.

7b You _____ (have to) even when it's raining.

Consolidation

5a Complete the job ad.

Part-time [1] j__ **offer**

We need people to [2] w_____ gardens. You [3] h_____ to be in good shape and must like working hard. You [4] d_____ have to have any special qualifications. ***Good money.***

Hours: 10 A.M. to 5 P.M. on Saturdays and Sundays

Please contact Mr. Williams@weeders.com

b Complete the conversation.

Rob: This looks interesting.

Adrian: Well, you'd [5] b_____ call quickly because I know a lot of people who are looking for part-time jobs.

Rob: Do you think I [6] o_____ to tell them that I'm going on vacation in three weeks?

Adrian: No, you'd better [7] n_____ tell them yet. Wait until they've hired you.

Rob: So, what [8] s_____ I say?

Adrian: Tell them that you love mowing your parents' [9] l_____ and really enjoy hard work. You [10] h_____ to show them that you're the best person for the job.

Extra challenge!

6 ★★★ Look at the signs and complete the sentences using the correct form of the verbs from the box.

- • 'd better • ~~don't have to~~ • must • must not
- • shouldn't

---

1 pay / get in

You don't have to pay to get in.

2 be / over 16 to enter the park

_____

3 carry / your money where people can see it

_____

4 bring / food or drink into the park

_____

5 get / to the park early if you want to enjoy your day

_____

3c   You can't make me stay at home.

Grammar: *make, let, allowed to*

1 ★ Circle the correct answers.

1 My mom _____ me clean my room every Saturday.

  a) lets   (b) makes)   c) allows

2 I'm _____ to stay up late on weekends.

  a) let   b) made   c) allowed

3 Are students in your school _____ to wear what they want?

  a) allowed   b) let   c) made

4 Our teacher _____ us stay late yesterday because we hadn't finished our work.

  a) made   b) allowed   c) let

5 Will your parents _____ you come to the concert with us on Friday night?

  a) make   b) let   c) allow

6 My dad _____ me watch TV before I do my homework but my mom doesn't.

  a) allows   b) lets   c) makes

2 ★★ Complete the text about Summerhill school with the correct form of the verbs in parentheses.

Summerhill school was opened in England in 1921. It looks like a traditional school, but it is very different. The students 1 *are allowed to decide* (allow/decide) how the school should be run and what the rules should be. The school

2 _____ (let) the students _____ (do) whatever they want as long as they don't hurt others. The teachers 3 _____ (not make) the students _____ (go) to classes; the students 4 _____ (allow/choose) which classes they attend.

Students and teachers have meetings three times a week. The students 5 _____ (allow/discuss) their ideas and are as important as the teachers. There are some things that the students 6 _____, (not/allow/do) but the punishments for breaking the rules are also decided by both teachers and students. For example, they 7_____ (not/let) a student _____ (leave) the school when everyone else 8 _____ (allow/go) out.

The British government does not always agree with the ideas at Summerhill, and it has, in the past, tried to 9 _____ (make) the school _____ (change) how it educates students. So far, the school has continued to do what it thinks is best.

22

Use your English: Invite, accept, and refuse with excuses

3 ★ Circle the correct answers.

Conversation 1

Mia: Do you **1** *(want)* / *like* / *love* to go to the movies tonight?

Sophie: I'd **2** *want* / *wish* / *like* to but I'm **3** *worried* / *afraid* / *nervous* I can't. It's my mom's birthday.

Mia: That's a shame. What **4** *for* / *about* / *of* tomorrow?

Sophie: That **5** *sounds* / *looks* / *feels* great.

Conversation 2

Liam: Can you come **6** *under* / *over* / *through* this afternoon?

Adam: Sure, I'd **7** *want* / *love* / *hope* to.

Liam: Good. I have to weed my grandparents' yard, and I need some help.

Adam: Oh . . . Well, I don't really **8** *want* / *love* / *hope* to weed today. Sorry. It's cold and starting to rain. Maybe tomorrow.

Liam: OK, fine. Have fun. Don't worry about me!

Consolidation

4 Complete the conversation with words from the box.

| • allowed • don't let • let (x2) • like • make • not allowed • unfair |

Mike: On our trip to Vancouver, we're going to stay in a bed and breakfast. I have some information here from the Internet. Look. I want us to decide where we're going to stay.

Lucy: Hillview sounds OK. You're **1** *allowed* to come in any time before midnight and they **2** _____ you use the kitchen if you want.

Allie: I don't **3** _____ it. They **4** _____ you pay for a week in advance. What if we don't like it?

Lucy: They'll give us our money back, won't they?

Allie: No, it says here that they won't.

Lucy: What? You mean that if you leave after one day, you have to pay for a week? That's so **5** _____ !

Allie: We could try Rose Cottage.

Lucy: No way. It says here that they **6** _____ you do anything. You're **7** _____ to come back after nine o'clock because they lock the doors.

Allie: Well, what about the White House?

Lucy: Let me see . . . Yes, that's great. Mike, we want to stay at the White House.

Mike: I don't think the President would **8** _____ us stay there!

3D Values for living

A refugee's story

Read

1 ★ Read the text about Wyclef Jean and number the paragraphs in the correct order.

A [3]

Most of this aid has come through the Yéle Haiti Foundation which, he created in 2004 with his cousin. *Yéle* means "a cry for freedom," and Yéle Haiti aims to help people in Haiti with small projects that can provide them with work, food, and somewhere to live. Wyclef wants Haitians to be able to live in their own country and not have to become refugees to survive.

B [ ]

Wyclef Jean was born in Haiti, a poor island in the Caribbean, in 1972. When he was nine years old, his family moved to the U.S. He grew up in New Jersey where he met Pras Michel, another Haitian, and Lauryn Hill, an African-American. Together, they formed a group in the mid-1990s. They called their band The Fugees, a short form of the word *refugees*, because all of their families had come to the U.S. to look for a better life.

C [ ]

Wyclef has had a lot of support for his foundation from other celebrities. Brad Pitt and Angelina Jolie attended the first anniversary party for Yéle Haiti. After an earthquake hit Haiti in January 2010, Yéle Haiti helped hurricane victims in many ways. It launched a job creation program in Haiti, donated medical equipment and food, cleaned the streets, and planted trees. Wyclef's story shows that people who leave their own country can sometimes give something back to help the people who are left behind.

D [ ]

The Fugees were hugely popular. Their second album, *The Score*, sold eighteen million copies worldwide. Wyclef went on to make solo albums and produce songs for other artists. He has also spent a lot of time giving humanitarian aid to his homeland.

New words and phrases

2 ★★ Match the new words (1–5) with the definitions (a–e).

1 hugely   a) for people
2 worldwide   b) help
3 humanitarian   c) very
4 aid   d) the place a person was born
5 homeland   e) all over the world

Comprehension

3 ★★ Read the text again and answer the questions.

1 When and where was Wyclef born?

   Wyclef was born in Haiti in 1972.

2 Who were the three members of The Fugees?

   _____

   _____

3 Why was the band called The Fugees?

   _____

   _____

4 What does *Yéle* mean and how does Yéle Haiti help people?

   _____

   _____

5 How did Yéle Haiti help after the 2010 earthquake?

   _____

   _____

Listen

4 ★ 🎧 (4) Listen to five people talking about their experiences and match the speakers to how they are feeling.

Speaker 1   a) confused
Speaker 2   b) proud
Speaker 3   c) angry
Speaker 4   d) sad
Speaker 5   e) excited

5 ★★ Listen again and decide which person said each sentence.

a) I've always wanted to see the places that my grandfather told me about. _____

b) I'd love to be able to visit them soon. _____

c) I can't believe how well she has done since we got here. _____

d) Why did I believe them? _____

e) It's lucky that the people are so kind because I couldn't do all this on my own. _____

Write

6a ★ Imagine you are Speaker 2. You are now on vacation in your grandfather's homeland, Jamaica. You have been there for one week. Think about these questions and use your imagination to make notes.

1 How did you travel there?

   _____

2 What was the trip like?

   _____

3 Are any of your grandfather's family still there? Do people remember him?

   _____

4 What have you done so far?

   _____

5 What has surprised you?

   _____

6 What are your plans for the rest of your vacation?

   _____

b ★★ On a separate sheet of paper, use your notes to write a letter to a friend telling him or her about your vacation.

Dear _____ ,

I'm having a _____ time here in Jamaica. It's a really

_____ place.

We arrived last week. The trip was . . .

The most fun I've had in a long time

Phrases

1 ★ Match the statements (1–5) with the responses (a–e).

1 I'm not sure I can do this.

2 Let's go to the fair. We might win something.

3 I'm going to play again.

4 I'm going to the beach. Are you up for it?

5 This game looks pretty difficult.

a) Oh, no you're not! It's my turn now.

b) No, it's really easy. Just throw the dart at the playing card.

c) Well, try. You won't know until you do.

d) Don't get too excited. The prizes aren't usually that great.

e) Yes, great. I'll just go and get my bathing suit.

Grammar: Present perfect with *already, before, never, ever, yet*

2 ★ Write sentences using the present perfect.

you / already / win / three / !
You've already won three!

we / not / try / this / yet
Come on! _____

_____

we / already / have / lunch
No way. _____

I / never / be / on it before
I don't know. _____

_____

your husband /ever / climb / a
wall like this / ? _____

I / never / see / him before
I don't know. _____

3 ★★ Complete the chat with the simple past or the present perfect form of the verbs in parentheses and the time expressions in the correct place.

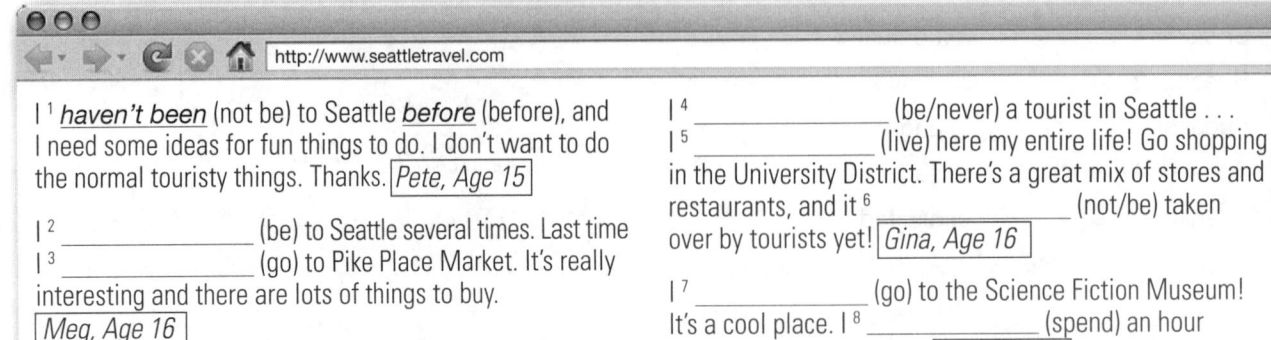

I ¹ *haven't been* (not be) to Seattle *before* (before), and I need some ideas for fun things to do. I don't want to do the normal touristy things. Thanks. [Pete, Age 15]

I ² _____ (be) to Seattle several times. Last time I ³ _____ (go) to Pike Place Market. It's really interesting and there are lots of things to buy. [Meg, Age 16]

I ⁴ _____ (be/never) a tourist in Seattle . . .
I ⁵ _____ (live) here my entire life! Go shopping in the University District. There's a great mix of stores and restaurants, and it ⁶ _____ (not/be) taken over by tourists yet! [Gina, Age 16]

I ⁷ _____ (go) to the Science Fiction Museum! It's a cool place. I ⁸ _____ (spend) an hour checking out one exhibit! [Pol, Age 14]

Grammar: Superlatives with the present perfect

4 ★★ Match the beginnings (1–6) to the endings (a–f). Then put the words in parentheses in the correct form.

1 What's ___the best___ (good) place

2 What's _____ (big) prize

3 What's _____ (delicious) food

4 What's _____ (good) video game

5 What's _____ (boring) book

6 Who's _____ (nice) person

a) you _____ (ever play)?

b) your mom _____ (ever read)?

c) you _'ve ever been_ (ever be) to?

d) you _____ (ever meet)?

e) your sister _____ (ever win)?

f) you _____ (ever eat)?

Use your English: React to good and bad news

5 ★ Complete the conversations.

1 **Max:** Guess what? My parents have just booked a vacation in New York for the summer. I'm so excited.

James: Congratulations! Wow! That's a _m a z i n_ g!

2 **Leo:** Oh, no! I forgot my homework.

Anna: That's t _ _ o b _ _ d.

3 **Ellie:** I can't believe it! I think someone stole my phone.

Mel: That's a _ _ _ l.

Harry: That's h _ _ _ _ _ _ _ e.

4 **Mia:** My parents don't allow me to go to parties during the week.

Sara: That's OK. C _ _ _ _ r _ p! I'm not allowed to go to parties during the week either.

5 **Jack:** Mom and Dad bought me an electric guitar for my birthday.

Victoria That's really c _ _ _ l!

Helen: A _ _ _ _ _ _ e! When can we come over to see it?

6 **William:** I won first prize in the school essay competition.

Charles: Good j _ b! You deserve it!

Harry: W _ _ _ t _ _ o! You worked really hard on your essay.

Consolidation

6 Complete the text with words or phrases from the box. Put the verbs in the simple past or the present perfect.

> • buy • do • ever • give • good job
> • most exciting • not leave • scratch • sell
> • ~~start~~ • wash • yet

Meet this week's
young entrepreneurs . . .

John Park and Jack Watson have always wanted to make money. They [1] ___started___ making money when they were eleven years old! What [2] _____ they _____ ? They [3] _____ cars! Now, at the age of eighteen, they are both successful businessmen and they [4] _____ school [5] _____ !

Today John and Jack don't wash cars. For the last year, they [6] _____ and sold electrical equipment. "We buy stuff cheaply that companies can't sell because somebody [7] _____ or damaged it," said John, "and then we sell it to other companies."

This year, they [8] _____ already _____ 800 TVs to a company in Spain. "It's the [9] _____ thing we've [10] _____ done," they said.

[11] _____ , boys! [12] _____ this story _____ you any ideas? Write to us with your ideas . . .

27

He's been playing for 10 years.

Grammar: Present perfect and present perfect continuous with *for* and *since*

1 ★ Complete the sentences using the present perfect or present perfect continuous with *for* or *since*.

They *have been playing* (play) together ____*for*____ 30 years.

We _____ (look) for Tom's house _____ three o'clock this afternoon. Let's stop and ask someone.

It's our anniversary. I _____ (go out) with Emma _____ a year.

It's broken. I _____ (have) only _____ it _____ Tuesday.

Where is she? We _____ (wait) here _____ four hours.

2 ★★ Complete the text with the present perfect or present perfect continuous. Use *for* or *since* where necessary.

Your questions about Miley Cyrus answered

Q: 1 How long / Miley / sing and act / ?
How long has Miley been singing and acting?

A: 2 She / act / she was nine

_____

3 She / sing / about six years

_____

Q: 4 Her best friends are Emily Osment and Mitchel Musso from *Hannah Montana*. how long / she / know them / ?

_____

A: 5 She / know / them / several years

_____

Q: 6 How long / she / be / friend / with Justin Gaston / ?

_____

A: 7 They / be / friends / he appeared on a reality TV show in 2008

_____

Grammar: Present perfect for numbers and amounts

3 ★ Complete the Quick star quiz on page 29 with the present perfect form of the verbs from the box.

• be • ~~make~~ • produce • score • sell • win

Quick star quiz

1 Q: How many albums _have_ Limp Bizkit _made_ ?
A: Five.
2 Q: How many Oscars _____ Meryl Streep
_____ ?
A: Two.
3 Q: How many CDs _____ U2 _____ ?
A: More than 145 million!
4 Q: How many people _____ in the band
Metallica since 2003?
A: Four.
5 Q: How many goals _____ David Beckham
_____ ?
A: I think it's over 100. I know he scored 62 for
Manchester United.
6 Q: How many songs _____ Eminem _____ ?
A: A lot. The best was "Renegade" by Jay-Z.

Vocabulary: Music words

4 ★ **Complete the crossword puzzle and find
the hidden word.**

1 Kanye West is a _____ _rapper_ _____ .

2 Mariah Carey writes her own songs. She's a
great _____ .

3 I think "Single Ladies" by Beyonce is a
great _____ .

4 Do you think U2 is a better _____
than Coldplay?

5 There are ten songs on our new _____ .

6 Look! We're number one on the _____ .

7 His first _____ sold really well online,
but nobody bought the entire album.

8 Robbie Williams is a great songwriter. The
_____ to his songs are always
interesting.

```
        ¹R A P P E R
²S      |   |   |
        ³S
   ⁴B
   ⁵A
        ⁶C
⁷S
     ⁸L
```

Kanye West

Consolidation

5 Circle the correct answers.

Conversation 1

Adrian: Who's your favorite **1** songwrite / (songwriter) /
singlewriter?

Meg: I like Amanda Ghost. She has **2** written / been
writing / wrote lots of great songs.

Adrian: Does she write the music and the **3** beats /
singles / lyrics?

Meg: Yes, I think so. She often writes for
other people.

Adrian: How long **4** has she written / did she write /
has she been writing for?

Meg: I'm not sure. She **5** sings / has sung / has been
singing **6** since / from / for the year 2000.

Conversation 2

Tom: How **7** many / long / much have you been
playing the guitar?

David: I bought my first one when I was eight so
8 I've been playing / I'm playing / I played it
for seven years.

Tom: How **9** much / many / long lessons have
you had?

David: About 300!

Tom: Do you want to be a famous musician?

David: Oh yes. I want to be number one on the
10 albums / charts / singles!

The website everyone is talking about

Grammar: Restrictive and nonrestrictive relative clauses

1 ★ Write R (restrictive relative clause) or NR (nonrestrictive relative clause).

1 This is the magazine that had a photo of me on the front cover last month. `R`

2 Tom Hayden, who's fifteen on Saturday, is going to have a party at his house. ☐

3 I'm looking for a book that is easy to read. ☐

4 Is this the store where you bought your cool shirt? ☐

5 We're going to Alnwick Castle, which was Hogwarts School in the Harry Potter movies. ☐

2 ★★ Circle the correct answers.

Websites for teens

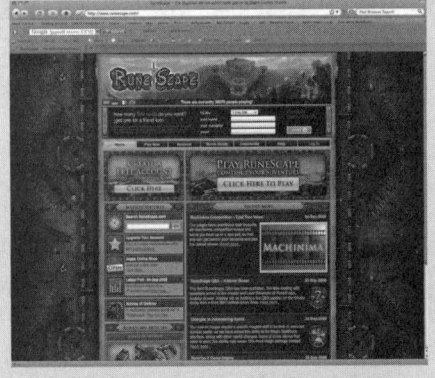

"Runescape," [1] *that /(which)/ who* is an online game that people can play alone or against other players, is a popular game for teenagers. It was created by Andrew Gower, [2] *who / that / whose* worked on it while he was in college. The game takes place in Gielinor, [3] *which / what / who* has different cities and countries in it. Players in Gielinor fight monsters or other players [4] *who / whose / which* are in the same place.

Teenagers [5] *who / what / whose* want to join a social networking site choose "Bebo." "Bebo" is a website [6] *where / which / that* teenagers can chat and design their own pages. New sections include "Bebo music" and "Bebo books," [7] *which / that / where* you can listen to music and read new books.

One of the things [8] *that / what / who* all teenagers have to do is school work. The public library, [9] *which / whose / who* website offers a huge range of things for all ages and interests, has the best educational resources. Go to www. . . .

3 ★★ Rewrite the sentences using the words in parentheses.

Andy: I just found a new social networking site. It's really good. (that)

1 I just found *a new social networking site that is really good*   .

Aaron: How did you hear about it?

Andy: Ryan Davies told me. His brother's in my class. (whose)

2 Ryan Davies, _____
_____.

Aaron: What's so special about this site?

Andy: There's a cool forum. You can post anything you want there. (where)

3 There's a cool forum _____
_____.

I was on one before. It wasn't as good as this one. (that)

4 I was _____
_____.

Aaron: I don't like putting my personal details on a webpage. Anyone can see them. (where)

5 I don't like _____
_____.

Andy: You can stop people from seeing your personal details if they aren't your friends (who)

6 Only people _____
_____.

Aaron: How many friends do you have on it?

Andy: I have only seven friends so far. It isn't many. (which)

7 I only have _____
_____.

I've only been on it a day.

Vocabulary: Phrasal verbs with *on*

4 ★ Look at the pictures and complete the words.

① You have to lo*g*_____ on to use this website.

② Can I t_____ these on, please?

③ You should p_____ a coat on.

④ H_____ on, I'll just go and get him.

⑤ Quick! T_____ on the TV! Our school is on the news today.

Consolidation

5 Complete the text with words from the box. Add commas where necessary.

> • count • hold • log • where • ~~which~~ • who
> • whose • which • who • whose

---

http://www.makeyourownwebsite.com

Do you want to make your own website? Do you have an idea ¹___*which*___ is going to make you rich? Well ²_____ on! We're here to give you advice. We have been working in the Web design business for more than twenty years. You can ³_____ on us!

We have more than 100 articles about starting a business ⁴_____ is more than any other website.

We have experts ⁵_____ advice is easy to read and always useful. They include our design consultant, Bob Portillo ⁶_____ own website won an award in 2009. Tim Rainer ⁷_____ has helped to design over a thousand websites, runs our help section. You will find special pages ⁸_____ you can see what your designs will look like.

If you are already a member, ⁹_____ on with your username and password below. People ¹⁰_____ aren't members can join by clicking **here**.

Extra challenge!

6 ★★★ Complete the sentences so they are true for you.

1 *Will Smith*, whose movies I really like, *is also a great singer*_____.

2 _____, who sits next to me in English, _____.

3 _____, which I bought last week, _____.

4 I'd like to go to a place where _____ _____.

5 I like people who _____ _____.

6 I know someone whose _____ _____.

INTEGRATED
CONSOLIDATION
SKILLS

English literature

Read

1 ★ Read the letter and write who wrote the books (1–3).

1 _____

2 _____

3 _____

Dear Parents,

The school year is almost finished, so I am writing to you about the English Literature 10th grade reading list for next year. All students should read these books during the summer vacation. After the vacation, we want to discuss the characters as well as the plots in class.

We have chosen these books for a number of reasons. *Animal Farm* is an important book in the history of English literature. I'm sure many students have read it already. George Orwell, who wrote many important books, used the idea of animals taking over a farm to discuss the real world. Students can read and enjoy it as a simple story about animals. During the school year, we will talk about the hidden message behind the story.

Journey to the River Sea, which is a new selection that both boys and girls will enjoy, was written by Eva Ibbotson in 2001. It is set in 1910 and will give students useful historical information about that time. What's more, the story includes excellent descriptions of journeys and different countries, which will help students with their own writing.

Framed is another new book for us this year. We have chosen this not only because it has a simple and interesting plot but also because the author, Frank Cottrell Boyce, is excellent at describing characters and the relationship between children and adults.

We are sure that both you and your child will be happy with the choice of books, which I'm sure will motivate all students to read and enjoy reading. If you have any comments or worries, please contact me at the school.

Yours truly,

Connor Peterson

Connor Peterson
Head of English

New words and phrases

2 ★★ Match the new words or phrases (1–5) with the definitions (a–e).

1 plot (n)

2 hidden message

3 set in

4 historical

5 to motivate

a) the real, not obvious meaning of a story

b) about the past

c) the place and time that the story happened in

d) what happens in a story

e) to make someone want to do something

Comprehension

3 ★★ **Read the letter again and circle the correct answers.**

1 The letter is to parents of children who ____.
   a) have already started 10th grade
   b) haven't finished 9th grade yet
   c) have just finished 9th grade

2 Last year, the school taught ____.
   a) none of these books   b) one of these books
   c) two of these books

3 During English lessons, students will discuss ____.
   a) the animals on *Animal Farm*
   b) what *Animal Farm* is really about
   c) Orwell's other books

4 *Journey to the River Sea* is ____.
   a) an adventure story   b) a history book
   c) a travel guide

5 The story in *Framed* is ____.
   a) complicated   b) easy to understand
   c) boring

Listen

4 ★ 🎧 5 **Listen to an English teacher talking to a class about a book and circle the correct answers.**

1 Name of the book this term: *Framed / Animal Farm*

2 It was the author's *first / second* book.

3 The book is set in *Liverpool / Wales*.

4 The hero of the book is a boy named *Manod / Dylan*.

5 ★★ **Listen again and complete the information.**

Author: Frank Cottrell Boyce

1 Born: In Liverpool in _____.

2 Number of books written: _____

3 Number of awards he has won: _____

4 He wrote *Framed* in _____.

5 Dylan's parents own a _____.

6 Dylan follows some _____.

7 The author got the idea from a story he read in _____.

Write

> **Writing tip: Conjunctions *as well as, what's more, not only . . . but also***
>
> **Remember!** We can combine two ideas in one sentence by using pairs of conjunctions,
> e.g. ***not only . . . but also***. We can add points with ***as well as*** and ***what's more***.
> *. . . we want to discuss the characters **as well as** the plot . . .*
> ***What's more**, the story includes excellent descriptions . . .*
> *We have chosen this **not only** because it has a simple and interesting plot **but also** because . . .*

6 ★ **Rewrite the sentences using the conjunctions in parentheses.**

1 We have to read a Shakespeare play and a book by Dickens this year. (as well as)
   This year we have to read a Shakespeare play as well as a book by Dickens.

2 These books are interesting and useful for our own writing. (not only . . . but also)
   _____
   _____.

3 I've read all Shakespeare's plays and I've seen five of them at the theater. (what's more)
   _____
   _____.

4 We're reading three books in English this year and learning how to write poetry. (as well as)
   _____
   _____.

7 ★★ **On a separate sheet of paper, write a review of a book you have read for school.**

Paragraph 1: Give a short summary of the book: the type of book, the author, where and when the story is set, and a short summary of what it is about.
Paragraph 2: Describe the characters and main events in the book.
Paragraph 3: Give your opinions about the book and reasons for them. Say how it made you feel.

For help with writing book reviews, go to the Writing bank on page 145 of your Student Book.

5A Unless they do something, . . .

Vocabulary: Landforms and the environment

1 ★ Circle the word that does not belong.

1 bush	tree	(river)
2 river	lake	desert
3 harbor	mountain	hill
4 island	valley	coast
5 field	waterfall	river

2 ★★ Match the numbers on the map with words in the box.

cliffs	8	coast	☐	forest	☐	harbor	☐
hill	☐	island	☐	lake	☐	path	☐

Grammar: Conditionals with *if*, *unless*, *provided that*, *as long as*

3 ★ Look at the information and circle the correct answers.

Welcome to Dreamworld

The resort that makes your dreams come true!

Open every day of the year*

**sometimes we need to close to clean the pools*

Sundays: **FREE**

Wednesdays: **Adults only**

Concerts: **Every Saturday night**

Free parking for guests ($20 a day for those without tickets)

1 a) We will be open every day of the year (unless)/ as long as we have to clean the pool.

   b) If we have to clean the pools, the resort *won't / will* be open.

2 a) If you *come / will come* on Sundays, you won't have to pay.

   b) You will have to pay *provided that / unless* you come on Sundays.

3 a) You can bring children to the resort *as long as / unless* you don't come on a Wednesday.

   b) There *will / won't* be children at the resort unless you come on a Wednesday.

4 a) *Provided that / Unless* you stay until Saturday evening, you will see one of our concerts.

   b) You won't see a concert if you *don't / won't* come to the resort on a Saturday.

5 a) You won't have to pay for parking *provided that / unless* you have a resort ticket.

   b) If you *don't / won't* have a ticket for the resort, you will have to pay $20 a day to park.

4 ★★ **Write the questions and answers. Use the conditional and the words in parentheses.**

Island Survivor

Fifteen young people will live on an island for fourteen weeks. You choose who goes each week.

Your questions answered . . .

Q: ¹ what / happen ⇨ they / get lost (if)
What will happen if they get lost?

A: ² they / not / get lost ⇨ do / what they are told (provided that)

_____

Q: ³ they / have to / leave the island ⇨ they / not do / what they're told (if)

_____

A: ⁴ they / not / have to leave ⇨ you / say "Go!" (unless)

_____

Q: ⁵ I / miss a show ⇨ I / be able / to see it later? (if)

_____

A: ⁶ you / be able to see it later ⇨ you / have Internet (as long as)

_____

Q: ⁷ how much / it / cost ⇨ I / call in (if)

_____

A: ⁸ it / cost / $1 a minute ⇨ you / use a cell phone (unless) . you / use a cell phone ⇨ it / cost / $1.50 a minute (if)

_____

_____

Consolidation

5 **Complete the e-mail with the correct form of the words from the box.**

> • do • have to • hill • if • ~~island~~ • lake • long
> • not go • provided • sleep • unless

From:	Meg
To:	Sara

Hi Sara,

Thanks for the e-mail about the rock festival in the park. It sounds great, but are you sure that the bands play on the ¹ _island_ in the middle of the ² _____? How will they get all their sound equipment there?

Do you really want to camp out Saturday night? I don't mind staying in a tent, but I ³ _____ camping ⁴ _____ there are toilets and showers! Do you think there will be somewhere nice to camp?

I'm worried about the weather, too. What ⁵ _____ we _____ if it rains? I ⁶ _____ in the tent ⁷ _____ that it's warm and dry. If it rains, I think we should go home for the night. It's not far and my dad will come get us ⁸ _____ we want. I hate sleeping in a wet tent!

I think that's all I'm worried about! Oh, sorry, one last question. If we go, ⁹ _____ we _____ buy tickets or is it free? I can pay for a ticket as ¹⁰ _____ as it isn't too expensive. If they're expensive, there's a ¹¹ _____ near the park. We could climb that and watch from the top!

Meg

Extra challenge!

6 ★★★ **Complete the sentences with landform words and then circle the correct answers.**

① 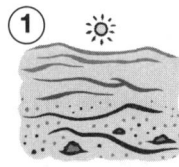 The biggest _desert_ in the world is the . . .
(a) Sahara. b) Gobi. c) Kalahari.

②  The highest _____ in the world is . . . Falls.
a) Niagara b) Victoria c) Angel

③  The highest _____ not in Asia is Mount . . .
a) Aconcagua. b) McKinley. c) Kilimanjaro.

④ The tallest _____ in the world is the . . .
a) oak. b) palm. c) redwood.

Vocabulary: Extreme weather and natural disasters

1 ★ Find ten more extreme weather and natural disaster words.

L	I	G	H	T	N	I	N	G	A
A	A	B	C	H	D	E	F	G	H
N	H	T	S	U	N	A	M	I	O
D	U	I	J	N	K	L	M	N	H
S	R	P	Q	D	R	S	T	S	A
L	R	U	V	E	W	G	X	T	I
I	I	T	O	R	N	A	D	O	L
D	C	Y	Z	A	B	L	C	R	S
E	A	D	E	I	G	E	F	M	T
J	N	K	N	H	L	O	M	P	O
H	E	A	T	W	A	V	E	S	R
Q	S	N	O	W	S	T	O	R	M

2 ★★ Complete the headlines with extreme weather or natural disaster words.

1. A_valanche___ in France
   Snow from mountain destroys twenty houses

2. B_____ in Chicago
   Roads closed because of wind and snow

3. D_____ in Australia
   There hasn't been rain here for two years

4. F_____ in Bangladesh
   Thousands lose their homes as water levels rise

5. Sudden d_____ in Seattle
   Six inches of rain fell in just two hours

6. E_____ in Greece
   Houses shook for five minutes; no serious injuries

7. F_____ in Africa
   UN brings in food to help starving people

Grammar: Future time clauses with *when, until, as soon as, by the time, before*

3 ★★ Complete the e-mail with the correct form of the verbs in parentheses.

To:	All tornado chasers
From:	Brad
Subject:	Tornado

Hi Guys,

The tornado should arrive tomorrow afternoon. Here's the plan.

Before the tornado 1 ___arrives___ (arrive), we 2 _____ (prepare) our equipment. As soon as we 3 _____ (see) the tornado, we 4 _____ (drive) towards it. We 5 _____ (film) the storm when we 6 _____ (get) close to it. Tornadoes move fast and by the time your camera 7 _____ (be) ready, the tornado 8 _____ (not be) in the same place. Take lots of photos and there'll certainly be some good ones. We 9 _____ (not leave) the area until the tornado 10 _____ (disappear) so eat before you leave home. Please don't bring food with you. Last time we got too close to a tornado in Kansas and our picnic ended up in Oklahoma!

Brad

4 ★★ Complete the messages with words from the box. Put the verbs in the correct form.

> • arrive • as soon as (x2) • before • until (x2)
> • by the time (x2) • not be • ~~not know~~ • tell

Rosy at 4:46 on June 10 wrote
Does anyone know about the volunteer work during vacation yet?

Terri at 4:59 on June 10 wrote
No. We **1** _won't know_ anything
2 _____ Kelly gets in touch.
3 _____ she e-mails me, I'll let you know.

Rosy at 5:06 on June 10 wrote
4 _____ Kelly e-mails, there
5 _____ any good jobs left. We'll have to clean toilets or something!

Kelly at 6:23 on June 14 wrote
Hi! I found us work for three weeks near Portland.

Terri at 6:31 on June 14 wrote
Great! What kind of work?

Kelly at 6:43 on June 14 wrote
Well, it's on a farm but we won't know exactly what we have to do
6 _____ the brochure **7** _____.

Rosy at 6:53 on June 14 wrote
Well, I hope it's OK. **8** _____ the brochure arrives, it'll be summer vacation! I want to find out as much as I can about the place and the work
9 _____ we go.

Kelly at 7:05 on June 14 wrote
Stop worrying, Rosy. I'll probably get it tomorrow. **10** _____ it arrives, I **11** _____ you all about it.

Consolidation

5 Circle the correct time expressions and then unscramble the letters to form words for extreme weather or natural disasters.

1 We want to go to Biloxi, but we won't go (until)/ _by the time_ the (ldofo) _flood_ water disappears.

2 We're going camping in Texas in August. There's a (heat veaw) _____ there now, but I just know that _until / as soon as_ Dad starts putting the tent up, there'll be a sudden (opnrdowu) _____!

3 We're going skiing in the Alps in two weeks, but there was an (nvclahaea) _____ there last week and they won't open the ski slopes _when / until_ they're sure it's safe.

4 We're going to Italy in August. There was an (hakuareqet) _____ there last November but, _as soon as / by the time_ we get there, everything will be normal again.

5 We'll either go to Florida in July, _until / before_ the (ruieahrnc) _____ season starts, or in December after it ends.

5c In case it gets cold

Phrases

1 ★ Circle the correct answers.

1 Adrian: Are you going to buy those hiking boots?

   Tim: I'd love to but I only have a twenty *to* / *(on)* / *for* me.

2 Man: Can I help you? What are you looking *for* / *in* / *up*?

   Tim: I'm interested in this camping stove but it's in its box and I can't see it.

   Man: I'll open it *out* / *off* / *up* for you, if you like.

3 Tim: Neil doesn't want to come camping with us because he can't live without a TV.

   Adrian: How *poor* / *sad* / *lonely* is that!

Grammar: *in case* + simple present

2 ★ Complete the conversation with the simple present form of the verbs in parentheses.

Joe: I'm all packed and ready to go to Greece. What's that?

Mom: Just a few things you might need. An umbrella, in case it **1** *rains* (rain). A blanket in case you **2** _____ (be) cold at night. A CD player in case your MP3 player **3** _____ (not work). A cook book in case you **4** _____ (not like) Greek food. Some batteries in case the stores **5** _____ (not sell) them. A Greek dictionary in case the people **6** _____ (not speak) English . . .

Joe: . . . and some money for a doctor in case I hurt my back with this heavy backpack!

3 ★★ Read the chat. Then rewrite the sentences using *in case* and the simple present.

Beth > Are you all ready for the concert tomorrow night?

Angie > **1** Yes. I'm going to do all my homework tonight because I might be too tired on Sunday.

Beth > **2** Me too. I'm going to read my English notes too because we might have a surprise test on Monday.

Angie > **3** I'm going to get my tickets on the Internet tonight because there might be a long line tomorrow.

Beth > Good idea. What about money? How much are you going to take?

Angie > **4** I'm going to take some money for a cab because we might miss the last bus.

Beth > What about money for food?

Angie > **5** I'm going to take sandwiches because there might not be any food there.

Beth > Do you think we'll meet Robbie?

Angie > I don't know. I think **6** I'll take a CD because he might come out to sign autographs after the concert.

B: Are you all ready for the concert tomorrow night?

A: **1** Yes. I'm going to do all my homework tonight *in case I'm too tired on Sunday* _____ .

B: **2** Me too. I'm going to read my English notes too _____ _____ .

A: **3** I'm going to get my tickets on the Internet tonight ____ _____ .

B: Good idea. What about money? How much are you going to take?

A: **4** I'm going to take _____ _____ .

B: What about money for food?

A: **5** I'm going to _____ _____ .

B: Do you think we'll meet Robbie?

A: I don't know. I think **6** I'll _____ _____ .

Vocabulary: Camping equipment

4 ★ Look at the pictures and complete the words.

Things to take

Sleeping and other things

A  **1** <u>tent</u>, a good  **2** s_____

b_____ to keep me warm, a strong

 **3** b_____ to carry everything in, and a

 **4** f_____ for the nighttime.

Food

A  **5** c_____ s_____ to cook on,

 **6** m_____ to light it with, and a

 **7** p_____ to cut bread.

Problems

Some  **8** i_____ r_____ to stop things from

biting me and  **9** b_____ in case I cut myself.

Use your English: Make and respond to requests

5 ★ Circle the correct answers.

Tom: Could I **1** (borrow) / lend / give ten dollars from you? I want to buy a penknife and a flashlight.

Leo: **2** True / Sure / Really, here you are.

Tom: That's terrific. I'll **3** lend / borrow / give it back tomorrow.

Ray: Could you **4** take / get / borrow me some things from the store?

Liam: Yes, of **5** sure / fine / course.

Ray: Thanks. I'll **6** do / make / have the same for you one day.

Natalie: Could you **7** borrow / take / lend me your homework? I haven't done it.

Cathy: I **8** not / can't / like.

Natalie: OK. It doesn't **9** mind / matter / worry. I'll ask Amelia.

Consolidation

6 Complete the signs with the names of the objects and the correct form of the verbs from the box.

> • come • ~~get~~ • need
> • not have • not like

①  Take a <u>can opener</u> in case you <u>get</u> bored eating in expensive restaurants.

②  Buy our _____ in case the sun _____ out (it can happen, even in San Francisco!)

③  Take a box of _____ in case you _____ to light a fire.

④ 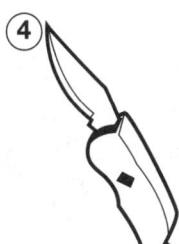 Take a _____ in case the campsite restaurant _____ clean knives.

⑤  Buy our super strong _____ in case you _____ your campsite and you have to walk to another one.

Glaciers

Read

1 ★ Read and complete the text with the sentences (a–e).

a) A lot of people were hurt.

b) No one knows exactly how close it was.

c) The sea here is home to seals, walruses, and whales.

d) In all that time, there had never been an accident before.

e) They were looking at the glacier above their heads.

> **Learning strategy: Dictionary skills (2)**
> **Remember!** When you look up a word in a dictionary, look at the example sentences to see the different meanings of the word in context.

Cruises to the Arctic are becoming more and more popular. Because of global warming, there isn't much ice and it is easier for boats to sail. One popular place to visit is the Svalbard Islands, 310 miles north of Norway. ¹ _c_

In 2007, fifty tourists were traveling on the boat, the *Alexey Maryshev*. ² ___ Suddenly, a large piece of ice broke off and crashed down into the sea. There was a huge wave, and pieces of ice went everywhere. The ship rolled because of the wave and people fell on the deck. ³ ___ Doctors treated some of the injured people on the boat and a helicopter took three people to a hospital in Tromso, Norway.

Luckily, the boat was not damaged and sailed back to the capital of the islands, Longyearbyen. People on the boat said that it had sailed too close to the glacier. ⁴ ___ First reports said 229 feet, then 164, and some people even say it was just 50 feet from the ice.

The tour was organized by the British tour company, Discover the World. It has been organizing trips to the Arctic for twenty years. ⁵ ___ A spokesperson said that the tourists on the boat were looking for adventure and excitement. They certainly got that!

New words and phrases

2 ★★ Circle the correct meaning (a or b) for the new words or phrases (1–4) as they are used in the text.

1 break off
   a) to separate from something suddenly
   b) to end something suddenly
2 wave
   a) a large wall of water in the sea
   b) to signal "hello" or "good-bye" by moving the hand back and forth

3 roll
   a) a small loaf of bread for one person
   b) to move from side to side so that one side is higher than the other
4 treat
   a) to give medical help to a person
   b) to pay for someone to have a good time

Comprehension

3 ★★ Write T (true), F (false), or DK (don't know).

1 It is easier to sail to the Arctic now because there is less ice in the sea. `T`

2 When the ice crashed into the sea, fifty people were standing on the boat's deck. ☐

3 The ice crashed onto the boat. ☐

4 People fell because the boat rolled. ☐

5 The captain had planned to sail to Longyearbyen before the accident happened. ☐

6 It is impossible to say for certain how close to the glacier the boat was. ☐

7 It wasn't the first time that a Discover the World tour had had an accident. ☐

Listen

4 ★ 🎧 6 Listen to Donna and Mark who were on the *Alexey Maryshev*. Write D (Donna) or M (Mark).

1 Who wasn't on deck at the time? ☐

2 Who fell on some stairs? ☐

3 Who had just seen a whale? ☐

4 Who had a cell phone? ☐

5 Who needed a bandage? ☐

5 ★★ Listen again and circle the correct answers.

1 Donna was in her room because she was ____.

a) tired   b) cold   c) hungry

2 When Donna heard the bang she wanted to ____.

a) go to her room   b) go to the deck

c) stay where she was

3 Donna fell on the stairs because ____.

a) the boat was moving

b) she was running too quickly

c) there was ice on the stairs

4 Mark took pictures of the whale on ____.

a) his cell phone only

b) a camera and a cell phone

c) his camera only

5 Mark read about polar bears ____.

a) before he got on the boat

b) while he was on the boat

c) on the islands

6 Donna needed a bandage for her ____.

a) head   b) arm   c) knee

Write

6 ★ Complete the fact card with the information from the box.

> • Longyearbyen • Norwegian • 37,900mi²
> • 310 miles north of Norway
> • polar bears, reindeer, arctic foxes • 2,321

The Svalbard Islands

Position:	¹ *310 miles north of Norway*
Area:	² _____
Biggest island:	Spitsbergen
Capital city:	³ _____
Language:	⁴ _____
Population:	⁵ _____
Money:	Norwegian krone
Work:	Tourism, technology, research, mining
Animals: Land:	⁶ _____
Sea:	whales, dolphins, seals, walruses
Air:	many kinds of sea birds

7 ★★ On a separate sheet of paper, use the information in Exercise 6 to write a fact sheet about the Svalbard islands. Use these headings and ideas:

Where are the islands and how big are they?
Who lives there and what do they do?
What animals can you see there?

If I were invisible for a day, . . .

Imagination

6

Grammar: Conditional: *if* clause + past

1 ★ Complete the text with the conditional form of the verbs in parentheses.

```
http://www.friendsfound.com
```

friends ▪ found   **Home**   **Profile**   **Friends**   **Inbox**

What would you do?

Compare your ideas with your friends!

Where [1] *would you travel* (you/travel) to if you [2] _____ (have) a time machine? If you [3] _____ (want) to meet a famous person, you [4] _____ (can go) back in time or you [5] _____ (may prefer) to see what the future looks like. It's your choice! If time travel [6] _____ (be) possible, you [7] _____ (may like) to see someone famous in concert like The Beatles or Elvis.

Which band would you want to see? You might not want to travel in time. If you [8] _____ (can see) any band you wanted, you [9] _____ (may choose) to get a ticket to see your favorite band playing now. Or here's another idea. If you [10] _____ (travel) to the future, you [11] _____ (can find out) who will be popular next year. You [12] _____ (can tell) all your friends about this awesome band you know. They'll be amazed next year when the band you told them about becomes really famous!

---

2 ★★ Complete the texts with the correct form of the verbs from the box.

> • become • ~~can play~~ • can manage • choose • join • know • make
> • may become • practice • tell

```
http://www.friendsfound.com
```

friends ▪ found   **Home**   **Profile**   **Friends**   **Inbox**

If you could have one ability, what ability would you choose?

Matt wrote: I'd like to be able to play the guitar. If I [1] *could play* the guitar, I [2] _____ a band. If we [3] _____ a lot, we [4] _____ famous. If we [5] _____ famous, we [6] _____ lots of money.

Comments (2)

Steve wrote: OK, Matt, so if you were in a band, I [7] _____ the ability to make money and to be a good businessman. If I [8] _____ how to make money, I [9] _____ your band!

Matt wrote: But if you were our manager, you [10] _____ us what to do. I wouldn't like that!

Vocabulary: Transitive phrasal verbs

3 ★ **Check (✓) the correct sentences and cross (✗) the incorrect sentences.**

1 a) Let's check out the new sports store. ✓
  b) Let's check the new sports store out. ✓
  c) Let's check it out. ✓
  d) Let's check out it. ✗

2 a) Pick that trash up. ☐
  b) Pick up that trash. ☐
  c) Pick it up. ☐
  d) Pick up it. ☐

3 a) We should turn off the TV now. ☐
  b) We should turn it off now. ☐
  c) We should turn off it now. ☐
  d) We should turn the TV off now. ☐

4 a) Can you give me back my book, please? ☐
  b) Can you give back me my book, please? ☐
  c) Can you give me my book back, please? ☐
  d) Can you give it back, please? ☐

4 ★ **Circle the correct answers.**

1 Have you ever asked anyone (out)/ off / in?

2 Come in and take on / up / off your coat.

3 How often do your parents tell you to turn over / down / out your music?

4 Did you find off / out / up when the class starts?

5 Make sure you put off / on / down a jacket when you go out. It's freezing.

5 ★★ **Complete the sentences with one word from each box. Put the verbs in the correct form. There is an extra word in each box.**

• find • pick • turn • turn • ~~turn~~	• ~~off~~ • on • out • up • up

1 Are you watching TV again? _Turn_ it _off_ and go outside for some fresh air.

2 Did you _____ _____ what Joe was up to last night?

3 Can you _____ _____ the radio? I like this song but I can't hear it.

4 Quick! _____ _____ Channel 9 news. There's a story about our school.

5 We cleaned the school playground yesterday. I _____ _____ 27 candy bar wrappers!

Consolidation

6 **Complete the conversation with the correct form of the words from the box.**

• check • should • find • if • might • not have • ~~out~~ • say • talk • wouldn't

Nick: There's Lisa again. She's so cool. Why don't you ask her 1 ___out___?

Dan: I'm still thinking about Amy.

Nick: Amy! She's history! 2 _____ you asked Lisa out, you would forget Amy.

Dan: If I 3 _____ to Amy, she 4 _____ go out with me again.

Nick: No, she 5 _____. Amy's with Chris now. Forget Amy. Lisa's really nice. If I 6 _____ a girlfriend, I'd ask her out. Why don't you 7 _____ out if she's busy this weekend?

Dan: Where 8 _____ I take her if she 9 _____ yes?

Nick: You could 10 _____ out the new restaurant in the shopping center.

Dan: OK, here I go. Wish me luck. Um . . . Lisa . . .

Phrases

1 ★ **Complete the conversations with phrases from the box.**

> • Come on • Hands off • See you in

Rob: OK. I got two DVDs for $12. So, that's $4 each for you, me, and Annie.

Alex: But we only agreed to get one DVD. I have to be home by 10:30 P.M. I won't be able to watch both of them.

Annie: Me too. We'll give you $2 each, Rob, not $4!

Annie: Rob's house is this way.

Alex: I know. I'm just going to get some pizza. 1 _____ a few minutes.

Rob: Mmm, that pizza smells good.

Alex: 2 _____! This is mine. I'm starving.

Annie: Rob, these DVDs are awful. Turn off the TV, I'm going to throw them in the trash, where they belong!

Rob: 3 _____, they're not that bad!

Grammar: *wish/if only* + simple past

2 ★ **Write sentences with *wish* or *if only* and the simple past.**

> ▽ | ▁ ▬ ✕
>
> ## Things wrong with my life
>
> **Appearance:** [1] too short
> **Personality:** [2] too shy
> **Possessions:** [3] no MP3 player
> [4] really old computer
> **Abilities:** [5] not very good at singing
> **Friends:** [6] don't know many people here
> [7] have to come home very early in the evening
> **School work:** [8] always get bad grades
> [9] My mom worries about me all the time
>
> . . . but Maria e-mailed today and she wants to meet on Saturday! Maybe there's nothing wrong with my life after all.☺

1 I _____*wish I was*_____ taller.

2 If _____ so shy.

3 I _____ an MP3 player.

4 If _____ so old.

5 I _____ sing better.

6 If _____ more people here.

7 I _____ to come home so early at night.

8 If _____ better grades in school.

9 I _____ about me so much.

3 ★★ **Write the sentences and then match them to the correct people in the pictures on page 45.**

1 wish / be / at the beach

_____*I wish I was at the beach.*_____ D

2 only / can / play the guitar

_____

_____

3 wish / not be / so tired

_____

_____

_____

4 only / know / what the teacher / is / talking about

_____

_____

_____

5 wish / be / four o'clock

_____

_____

_____

6 only / not have to / wear school uniform

_____

_____

_____

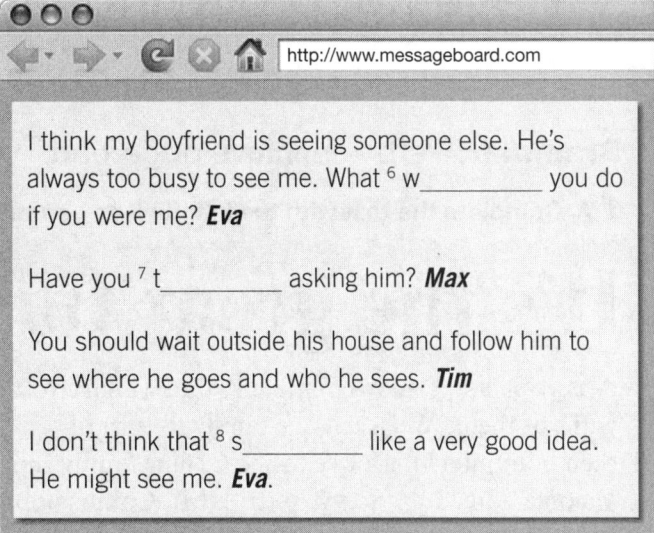

I think my boyfriend is seeing someone else. He's always too busy to see me. What ⁶ w_____ you do if you were me? **Eva**

Have you ⁷ t_____ asking him? **Max**

You should wait outside his house and follow him to see where he goes and who he sees. **Tim**

I don't think that ⁸ s_____ like a very good idea. He might see me. **Eva**.

Use your English: Ask for and give advice

4 ★ Complete the messages.

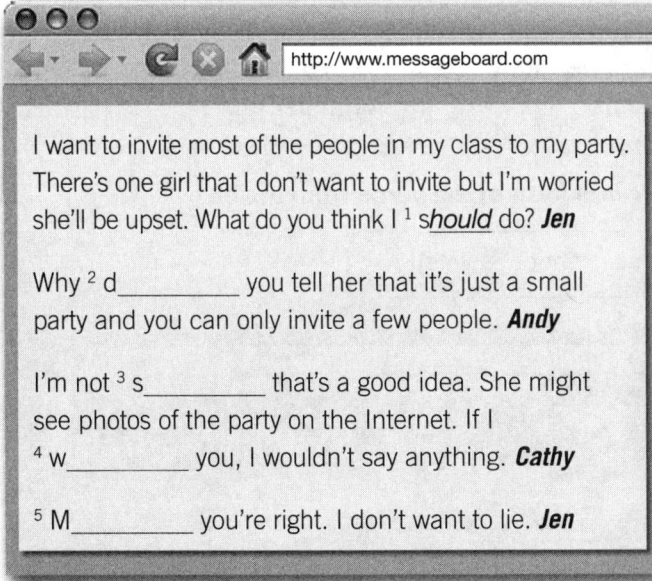

I want to invite most of the people in my class to my party. There's one girl that I don't want to invite but I'm worried she'll be upset. What do you think I ¹ s*hould* do? **Jen**

Why ² d_____ you tell her that it's just a small party and you can only invite a few people. **Andy**

I'm not ³ s_____ that's a good idea. She might see photos of the party on the Internet. If I ⁴ w_____ you, I wouldn't say anything. **Cathy**

⁵ M_____ you're right. I don't want to lie. **Jen**

Consolidation

5 Circle the correct answers.

Harry: I wish I **1** *have /* (*had*)/ *am having* a better cell phone.

Nathan: Yours is all right.

Harry: But it doesn't have a camera and I can't listen to music on it.

Nathan: **2** *How / What / Why* don't you ask for a new one for your birthday?

Harry: **3** *It / That's / This* a good idea. I will.

Jack: A few of us are going for ice cream at La Dolce Vita in the mall. Do you want to come?

Stella: I'd love to. If only I **4** *don't / wouldn't / didn't* have to go to my piano lesson.

Jack: If I **5** *am / were / would be* you, I'd call and say you're sick.

Stella: **6** I'm *not sure / not right / not* knowing, that's a good idea.

Jack: OK.

Stella: Sometimes I wish I **7** *weren't / wouldn't be / aren't* so honest.

6B

45

Grammar: Verb + infinitive or gerund

1 ★ Complete the text with the infinitive or gerund (*-ing*) form of the verbs in parentheses.

It's the great turn off!

Are we all addicted to computers? Can we survive without them? We asked one family to turn off their computers for a week. The Collins family from Tacoma agreed ¹ _____to try_____ (try). Mr. Collins hoped ² _____ (have) more time to decorate the house. Mrs. Collins didn't mind ³ _____ (not use) the computer because she only uses it to e-mail friends. Fifteen-year-old Laura admitted ⁴ _____ (spend) a lot of time on the computer but denied ⁵ _____ (be) worried about not having one for a week.

So the question was . . . would the family manage ⁶ _____ (survive) for a whole week without their computers? As the week approached, they seemed ⁷ _____ (be) excited by the idea . . .

One week later, we visited the Collins family again. Did they survive? Mr. and Mrs. Collins enjoyed

⁸ _____ (do) other things. Laura found it more of a problem. She got bored quickly. When we suggested ⁹ _____ (continue) the experiment for a second week, she locked herself in her bedroom . . . with her computer on.

2 ★★ Complete the text with the infinitive or gerund (*-ing*) form of the verbs from the box.

• buy • go • like • make • manage • play • ~~read~~ • see • shoot • watch

Keep on playing ▪ ▫ ▪ ▫ ▪ ▫ ▪ ▫ ▪ ▫ ▪

Fourteen-year-old Tim Stone doesn't play video games. He enjoys ¹ _reading_, especially science-fiction books, and he plays the guitar. Tim agreed ² _____ two video games and tell us what he thought of them. Why did he agree?

"I wanted ³ _____ why everyone gets so excited about them. I didn't expect ⁴ _____ them. Sitting in front of a screen is really boring. I don't like ⁵ _____ TV or ⁶ _____ to the movies either."

So, what does he think now?

"I can't stand ⁷ _____ aliens. I'm not very good with the buttons. I kept ⁸ _____ mistakes or getting killed because I went the wrong way. I prefer slower games. I enjoyed ⁹ _____ a baseball team. In fact, I've decided ¹⁰ _____ a baseball management game. They only cost about $20. I want my team to get into the Champions League Final."

Vocabulary: Noun suffixes -ion, -ment, -ity, and -y

3 ★ Use the words in the box to write nouns with the endings given.

> • ~~able~~ • accurate • coordinate • difficult
> • improve • move • organize • real

-ion: _____, _____

-ment: _____, _____

-ity: ___ability___, _____

-y: _____, _____

4 ★★ Complete the texts with the noun form of the words in parentheses.

Time of Dreams IV ★

The only [1] *explanation* (explain) for this game is that the makers want to make some easy money. There's a good [2] _____ (possible) that people who enjoyed Time of Dreams III will buy this. Time of Dreams III was excellent. This game isn't. It's a big [3] _____ (disappoint). There's none of the [4] _____ (excite) or [5] _____ (imagine) in this new game. The only [6] _____ (similar) is the name.

Race Around the World ★★★★

I saw this new racing game online and I bought it because it looked interesting. I'm very pleased with my [7] _____ (decide) because it's great. There are four levels of [8] _____ (difficult) and it is excellent [9] _____ (entertain).

Star Collector ★★★

One for the eight- to eleven-year-olds. A journey of [10] _____ (discover) to the stars. Players earn points for [11] _____ (brave) and determination.

Consolidation

5 Complete the news stories with the correct form of the words in the boxes.

(1) EXCITE / LEAVE / REAL
Excitement on *Reality* TV show when a contestant refuses *to leave*!

(2) DISAPPOINT / GIVE / TRAVEL
Would you like _____ around the world? We have decided _____ away ten free tickets. Enter our competition now to avoid _____.

(3) CORRECT / HAVE / TELL
This is a _____ of a story in yesterday's paper. The story said that David Kristianson had had an argument with his wife and she had walked out of a restaurant. Both David and his wife, Natasha, deny _____ any arguments and would like us _____ their fans that they are happy together as always.

(4) BRAVE / LOOK / PLAY
Goalie Ted Colon, showed great _____ in last night's game when he continued _____ even after losing two teeth. After the game, Ted said, "I don't mind _____ strange, but I hope my wife isn't mad!"

Extra challenge!

6 ★★★ Complete the sentences so that they are true for you.

1 I would like _____

_____

2 I'm going to start _____

_____

3 I can't stand _____

_____

4 I have decided _____

_____

5 I don't want _____

_____

6 If I lived on a desert island, I would miss _____

_____

6D Values for living

The prom

Read

1 ★ Read the text quickly and decide who it is for.

a) Teachers   b) Parents   c) Students   d) Visitors

2 ★★ Read the text again and match the headings (a–d) to the correct paragraphs (1–4).

a) **Finding a date**   b) **Making an effort**   c) **No more!**   d) **On the big day**

1 c

Every year, our school puts on an end-of-year party. Every year, fewer people show up and it's less and less interesting. It's just . . . nothing special. Let's do something else this year!

2 ☐

Why don't we organize a prom this year? We've all seen them in movies. People really try hard to look good. They think about their clothes for months before the prom. Some people buy or **rent** their clothes. But you can look good in something you've borrowed or even made. The girls look very glamorous in long dresses. The boys look really cool in black suits, white shirts, and even **bow ties**.

3 ☐

However, if people didn't have a date, they might not want to go. But I have an idea! Everyone without a date could write their name on a piece of paper. Then we would collect the names and take a name from the boy's bag and a name from the girl's bag and those two people would go to the prom together.

4 ☐

On the day of the prom, the school will be like Hollywood. We'll have a red carpet outside the front of the school. People will arrive in big **limousines**. Everything will be really glamorous and exciting. I'm not sure our town has many limousines, but we could try to organize something. Then, at the prom, there will be a band, not just a DJ, and a mixture of music so that people have to learn "real" dancing.

I'm sure people would love the idea, and it wouldn't cost the school much. Please sign my **petition** if you agree with me.

We want a prom!

1 Lucy Davies
2 Beth Simpson
3 Dan Wilkins

New words and phrases

3 ★★ Label the pictures with the words or phrases in bold in the text.

① ____bow ties____   ② _____   ③ _____   ④ _____

48

Comprehension

4 ★★ **Read the text again and circle the correct answers.**

What does the writer think about . . .

1 end-of-year parties?
   (a) They're not exciting.) b) They're a great idea.
   c) They're very popular.

2 end-of-year proms? They're good because . . .
   a) they're expensive.
   b) people care about them.
   c) you can see them in movies.

3 the problem of people without dates?
   a) It doesn't worry her.
   b) There is nothing she can do about it.
   c) She might know how to solve it.

4 Hollywood?
   a) It's a glamorous, exciting place.
   b) We don't know.
   c) She doesn't like it.

5 the music at proms?
   a) She prefers only DJs.
   b) She likes a mixture.
   c) She's not sure what kind of music there is.

Listen

5a ★ **Match the words with the headings.**

• ask out • boyfriend • color • CDs • dates • DJ • dresses • formal • girlfriend • going out • leather jacket • relaxing • styles • tie • waltz

Someone to go with	What to wear?	Proms or parties?
boyfriend		

b ★ 🎧 7 **Now listen. Which words from Exercise 5a do you hear?**

6 ★★ **Listen again and complete the sentences.**

Speaker 1

1 The prom is in _____ months.

2 The boy she likes is tall and _____, and he can _____.

Speaker 2

3 Girls can choose the length, _____, and _____ of their dresses.

4 He might not be allowed into the prom if he wears jeans and a _____.

Speaker 3

5 He doesn't want to look _____ at a party because he has to wear a _____ every day.

6 At the old school parties, no one worried about what they _____.

Write

7 ★★ **You are the writer of the poster in Exercise 1. On a separate sheet of paper, write an informal letter to your cousin in Los Angeles whose school has a prom every year. Use the Writing bank on page 146 of your Student Book and the plan below to help you write the letter.**

Paragraph 1: Start your letter
• Greet your cousin
• Ask how she is
• Tell her your news

Paragraph 2: Explain why you are writing
• Your idea for a prom
• The reasons you think it's a good idea
• Ask her about food, decoration, and speeches

Paragraph 3: End the letter
• Thank your cousin
• Say good bye
• Give best wishes

He asked me if I had a website.

Phrases

1 ★ Complete the conversations with phrases from the box.

> • actually • ~~Let me guess~~ • Well
> • Thanks for calling back

Greg: Oh, Mr. Davies. There was something I had to tell you . . . um . . .

Mr. Davies: 1 *Let me guess*. Someone called and you lost the message.

Greg: Not lost. I wrote her name down somewhere.

Mr. Davies: Somewhere? Do you think you can find it?

Greg: Here it is. It was Natalie Herrera who called.

Mr. Davies: Oh, good. Pass me the phone . . . Natalie, hi. It's Colin Davies.

Natalie: Colin! Hi! 2 _____ . I was worried you wouldn't get my message. The boy who answered the phone sounded a little confused.

Mr. Davies: 3 _____ , 4 _____ I almost didn't get it. Greg's not the best worker. Anyway, let's not worry about him. What did you call about?

Grammar: Reported statements and questions

2 ★ Complete the sentences with the correct form of the verbs in parentheses.

My name's Bond. James Bond.

1 James Bond said that his name ___was___ (be) Bond. James Bond.

I'll be back.

2 The Terminator said that he _____ (be) back.

Why are you saying good bye?

3 Troy asked Gabriella why she _____ (say) good bye.

I hate snakes!

4 Indiana Jones said that he _____ (hate) snakes.

3 ★★ Complete the sentences with direct or reported speech.

1 **Mark:** "I don't understand my homework."

Mark said *that he didn't understand his* _____

homework _____ .

2 **Lisa:** "I wasn't late last night."

Lisa said _____

_____ .

3 Jake: "_____

_____ "

Jake said that he had never seen that game before.

4 Erin: "Does Dan have my MP3 player?"

Erin asked _____

_____ .

5 Fran: "Who ate my sandwiches?"

Fran asked _____

_____ .

6 Angie: "_____

_____ "

Angie asked if I could look at her laptop.

4 ★★ **Read the notes and complete the police officer's report.**

Stolen laptop

Owner: Leo Morales

Interview by Police Offcer Matthew Henderson

MH: When did you lose the laptop?

LM: Saturday, May 16 at about 2 P.M.

MH: Where was the laptop?

LM: In a bag in The River View café.

MH: Do you often take your laptop there?

LM: Yes, I usually take it there on Saturdays. There's free Internet in the café.

MH: Can you remember who was in the café when you went to the bathroom?

LM: No, I can't.

I interviewed Leo Morales about a stolen laptop. First, I asked him when 1 _he had lost his laptop_ . He told me that he 2 _____ on Saturday, May 16 at about 2 P.M. I asked him 3 _____, and he told me that it 4 _____ in The River View café. I then asked him 5 _____ his laptop to the café. He said that he 6 _____ free Internet access there. I asked Leo 7 _____ who had been in the café at the time, but he said that 8 _____ . I then . . .

Use your English: Phone messages

5 ★ **Complete the words.**

Voicemail: Hello, you've 1 r <u>e a c h e d</u> Beth Smith. I'm sorry, I can't 2 t _ _ _ _ y _ _ _ _ call right now. Please 3 l _ _ _ e a message after the 4 t _ _ e, and I'll get back to you as soon as I can.

Meg: Hello, Beth. This is Meg. I was just calling to 5 c _ _ _ t. Can you 6 c _ _ l me when you get this 7 m _ s _ _ _ e?

Voicemail: Hello. This is Meg Thompson. I'm 8 s _ _ _ _ y I can't take your call right now but leave a message and I'll get 9 b _ _ k to you.

Beth: Hi, it's Beth. I got your message. I have my phone on now so 10 g _ _ e me a call soon.

Consolidation

6 Circle the correct answers.

Matt

Debbie called. She said that she 1 has / (had) called twice but you 2 didn't get / hadn't gotten back to her. She asked 3 are you / if you were all right. I 4 said / told her that you 5 had gone / have gone out and had left your phone at home. I said that you 6 will / would be back at about nine.

Matt

Debbie called again. She said that she 7 is / was going to bed early so she might not be awake when you get home. She 8 said / told that she 9 hasn't gotten / didn't have any important news but just 10 wanted / wants to chat.

Matt

Debbie called (again)! She wanted to know if you 11 can / could send her the link to the website you 12 told / said her about at school. Can you tell your friend that I'm your sister not your secretary?

Grammar: Reporting verbs

1 ★ Match the sentences (1–10) with the verbs (a–l). There are two extra verbs.

1 Can you help me with this homework?
2 Would you like to come to my party?
3 I won't be late again, honestly.
4 I can help you clean up if you want.
5 I'm not wearing that shirt!
6 Yes, it's true. I copied my homework from the Internet.
7 I didn't write anything on the school wall.
8 I'm sorry I forgot your birthday.
9 This burger is disgusting. It's cold and hard.
10 You should take up a sport or go to a gym.

a) admit
b) apologize
c) ask
d) complain
e) deny
f) explain
g) invite
h) keep
i) offer
j) promise
k) refuse
l) suggest

2 ★★ Report what the singer said using verbs from the box.

> • admit • apologize • complain • deny • promise • refuse

1 I'm sorry I didn't show up at the concert yesterday.

2 The newspaper reviews of my last album were very unfair.

3 It's not true. I'm not making an album with Eminem.

4 Yes, it's true. I have some personal problems.

5 Next year, I'll play more concerts in Seattle.

6 No, I won't join Take This again. No way!

At singer William Fulton's press conference yesterday, he . . .

1 _apologized for not showing up at the concert the previous day_ .

2 _____
_____ .

3 _____
_____ .

4 _____
_____ .

5 _____
_____ .

6 _____
_____ .

Consolidation

3 Write reported sentences.

Pete: Did you read the interview with the Brazilian soccer player, Jose Pepe?

Tim: No, what did he say?

Pete: Well, . . .

1 said / regret / go / home to Brazil / without telling his manager

He said he regretted going home to Brazil
without telling his manager.

2 apologize / miss / practice / last week

_____

_____

3 promise / not / shout at the manager again

_____

_____

4 deny / leave / a nightclub at 4 A.M. the night before an important game

_____

_____

5 offer / pay back / half his wages for the season

_____

_____

6 complain / news reporters / always make up / stories about him

_____

_____

Extra challenge!

4 ★★★ Look at the five people. Match them to the correct reporting verbs (a–e) and write their names. Then report what each person said.

a) ~~Paula Sweet (deny)~~ d) Jake Norris (promise)
b) Ben Fisher (suggest) e) Sara Philips (complain)
c) Nick Tyler (apologize)

I don't love Jack.

1 *Paula Sweet denied loving Jack.*

Katie, I'll never leave you.

2 _____

Dave, I'm sorry that I broke your MP3 player.

3 _____

My boyfriend never gives me flowers!

4 _____

Let's go to the park.

5 _____

Vocabulary: Relationship words and phrases

1 ★ Complete the crossword puzzle.

Across

2 care _____ someone

4 be _____ to someone

6 get on someone's _____

7 have a good relationship _____ someone

8 _____ up with someone

Down

1 ___have___ an argument with someone

3 _____ someone like a child

5 get _____ someone

2 ★★ Complete the texts with relationship words and phrases.

Your problems answered

I get ¹ ___along___ well with a boy in my class, but I don't want to go ² _____ with him. He doesn't understand.
Mel

I met a girl at a party, and I ³ _____ in love
⁴ _____ her as soon as I saw her. I asked her
⁵ _____ , and she said "Yes." But now we're
⁶ _____ lots of arguments, and I'm worried that we're going to break ⁷ _____ soon.
Aaron

My older sister ⁸ _____ engaged to Joe on her eighteenth birthday. She's going to get married ⁹ _____ him this summer. He's ten years older than she is. I'm worried. I'm sure he's not right for her.
Phil

All the girls in my class ¹⁰ _____ me like their little brother. I hate it! I'm the same age as them.
Dave

Grammar: Subordinating conjunctions that show contrast

3 ★ Circle the correct answers.

1 (Although) / Despite / However I like my parents, they sometimes annoy me.

2 One girl in my class is really pretty and really smart. Although / However / Despite, she isn't very friendly.

3 My parents can be really strict during the school year. On the other hand / Although / In spite of, they give me a lot of freedom during vacations.

4 Despite / In spite / Although of being quite good looking, I can't get a girlfriend.

5 However / Although / Despite arguing all the time, my brother and I are very close.

6 Despite / In spite of / Although my boyfriend likes playing sports, he also spends a lot of time playing video games.

4 ★★ Link the sentences using the words or phrases in parentheses.

A movie you have to see

Eclipse is the third of four movies in the *Twilight Saga series*. The first was *Twilight* and second was *New Moon*.

1 *Twilight* didn't get very good reviews. It was really popular. (although)
  <u>Although Twilight *didn't get very good reviews, it was really popular.*</u>

2 *Eclipse* is a romance. Teenagers who don't like love stories will also enjoy it. (on the other hand)

   _____

3 The movie features vampires and werewolves. It's for all ages. (however)

   _____

4 I was disappointed with the dialogue. I thought the special effects were awesome. (although)

   _____

5 I didn't enjoy *New Moon* very much. I decided to go see *Eclipse* last week. (despite)

   _____

6 *New Moon* was disappointing. *Eclipse* is a lot better. (however)

   _____

Consolidation

5 Complete the texts with one word in each blank.

Your problems answered

Problem

My parents don't want me to grow up. I'm fifteen. I've always [1] gotten_____ along well with my parents but, now that I'm older, the things they say and do are starting to get on my [2] n_____. They still [3] t_____ me like a little boy. [4] D_____ explaining how I feel, nothing really changes. [5] A_____ they know that my friends all go out on the weekend, they say I have to stay at home. What should I do?

Our advice

Your problem is a very common one. Parents often drive their children crazy with their rules. On the other [6] h_____, they often expect their children to be quite mature. [7] H_____, I'm sure that they are only trying to do what they think is best for you. They [8] c_____ about you, which is very important. You say that you have a good [9] r_____ with them. Try explaining how you feel again and ask them what they are afraid of. Good luck.

Communication in the 21st century

Read

1 ★ Read the texts and match the people and things (1–3) with the information (a–f).

1 I use my cell phone to see in the dark . . . [c] [f]

2 Lily Allen . . . [ ] [ ]

3 Ashton Kutcher . . . [ ] [ ]

a) is a singer.
b) is an actor.
c) ~~is a Facebook group.~~

d) has one million followers.
e) has half a million friends.
f) ~~has half a million members.~~

① *I use my cell phone to see in the dark* is a Facebook group. Facebook groups can be serious or they can be fun. People join to tell the world about their interests and hobbies. *I use my cell phone to see in the dark* is for people who can't live without their cell phones. They use them as calculators, flashlights, clocks, . . . anything, even for talking to people! The group has over half a million members. These members write messages about their phones and upload photos. Why join? No reason at all. It's just fun.

② Lily Allen is one of England's most popular singers. Before 2005, she wasn't very well-known, despite having a contract with a record company. She decided to put her songs onto MySpace. Thousands of people heard them. Her popularity through MySpace led to magazine interviews and her record label finally realized that she could be a star. Thirty-two million people have now downloaded songs from her website and she has half a million "friends."

③ Ashton Kutcher is a famous American actor. He is married to Demi Moore but is also famous because of Twitter. People who Twitter write short messages, like a blog but much shorter. Anyone can become a follower and receive these messages automatically on their cell phones or computers. Ashton and the TV channel CNN were both trying to be first to get one million Twitter followers, and Ashton won. Why is Ashton so popular? One thing he said he would do is to give $100,000 to help fight malaria if he got a million followers first.

New words and phrases

2 ★★ Match the new words (1–4) with their meanings (a–d).

1 contract

2 upload

3 malaria

4 automatically

a) an illness common in hot countries caused when an infected mosquito bites you

b) for example, to transfer photos from a computer to the Internet

c) without thinking about what you are doing

d) a formal written agreement

56

Comprehension

3 ★★ **Read the texts again and write *T* (true),**
***F* (false), or *DK* (don't know).**

1 Facebook groups don't have to be about $\boxed{T}$
  serious things.

2 You can see five hundred photos of phones $\square$
  on the group's pages.

3 Lily Allen has only made one album. $\square$

4 She became popular after magazines started $\square$
  interviewing her.

5 No one had a million followers on Twitter $\square$
  before Ashton Kutcher.

6 CNN doesn't have a million Twitter followers. $\square$

Listen

4 ★ 🎧 **8** **Listen to the conversation and
answer the questions.**

1 Who is the boy talking to?

_____

2 Where is the boy?

_____

5 ★★ **Listen again and circle the correct
answers.**

1 The boy is _____.

  a) at home   b) calling from a cell phone

  c) calling from a computer

2 His mom thinks he has to pay for _____.

  a) using a webcam   b) the phone call

  c) using the computer

3 The first thing he tells his mom to do is to _____.

  a) click a button   b) open a webpage

  c) switch on a webcam

4 The boy's hair is a mess because _____.

  a) it's a windy day   b) he hasn't washed it

  c) he's copying Mario's style

5 His mom wants to turn off the phone link
  because _____.

  a) she is going out to Mrs. Parker's house

  b) she doesn't have time to talk

  c) she doesn't want Mrs. Parker to see what her
  son looks like

Write

> **Writing tip: *First*, *second*, and *last***
>
> **Remember!** Use these words to list points.
>
> *There are several reasons. **First**, I have much
> more contact with my children.*
>
> ***Second**, my kids keep in touch with their
> grandparents via e-mail.*
>
> ***Last**, the bill for the landline is much cheaper!*

6 ★ **Make sentences and then write the
sentences in the correct order.**

Why make phone calls from your computer?

- an / very / Internet / it's / easy / Second, / to /
  phone / use

- webcam / speaker / see / a / can / if / Last, / he or
  she / the / you / other / has

- a / make / another / First, / phone / from / one /
  to / free / it's / call / to / computer

1 _____

  _____

2 _____

  _____

3 _____

  _____

7 ★★ **Write a blog about your favorite way
of communicating with your friends. Use *first*,
second, and *last* to separate your reasons.**

Vocabulary: Adjectives of emotion

1 ★ Circle the word that does not belong.

1 anxious	nervous	(calm)	4 sad	amused	lonely
2 scared	annoyed	frightened	5 embarrassed	shocked	ashamed
3 afraid	terrified	bored	6 thrilled	excited	worried

2 ★★ Complete the sentences with one adjective from each pair in the box.

> • bored/boring • confused/confusing • depressed/depressing
> • ~~excited/exciting~~ • frustrated/frustrating • terrified/terrifying

Tom was very _excited_ when his ticket for the rock concert arrived.

This ride is _____ but great!

Luis was very _____ by all the ropes.

Emma was very _____ when she broke up with Charles.

I'm lost! I wish I had a map. This is so _____!

The book was very _____, but Jan had to read it for school.

Grammar: *so* + adjective/adverb *(that)* . . . , *such a/an* + adjective + noun *(that)* . . . , *so many/much* + noun *(that)* . . . , Verb + *so much (that)* . . .

3 ★ Circle the correct answers.

Dear Sophie,
Greetings from Spain! I'm having ¹ (so)/such much fun. It's ² so/such a beautiful place and the weather is ³ so/such hot, I don't want to come home! Yesterday, we went to an old castle. It was ⁴ so/such old that there were only a few walls left. Today we are on the beach, which is great!
The food here is delicious. I've eaten ⁵ so/such much that I can't get my pants on! The first night, we found a nice restaurant. They have ⁶ so/such a big selection that we've been back every day.
Whoops, I've written ⁷ so/such much that there's no more room on the card.

Love, Katie

4 ★★ **Combine the sentences using the words in parentheses.**

Ashley: Hi, Marlon. How was Moscow?
Marlon: Great.
1 It was very interesting. I'd like to go back. (so)
It was so interesting that I'd like to go back.
Ashley: Did you buy any cool stuff?
Marlon: **2** We spent a lot on sightseeing. We didn't have any money for presents! (so)
No. _____
_____
Ashley: How did you get around town?
Marlon: By cab and subway.
3 Moscow is a very big city. You can't walk everywhere. (such)
_____
_____
Ashley: Did you have lunch out every day?
Marlon: No, it was too expensive.
4 However, we had huge breakfasts at the hotel. It didn't matter. (such)
_____
_____
Ashley: What did you do in the evening?
Marlon: Not much.
5 We were very tired at the end of the day. We usually had dinner and went to bed. (so)
_____
_____
Ashley: Did you learn any Russian?
Marlon: **6** Everyone spoke very quickly. I didn't understand anything. (so)
No. _____
_____
Ashley: Was Red Square beautiful?
Marlon: Yes, I thought so.
7 I took lots of photos. I ran out of memory on my camera! (so)
_____
_____
Ashley: Would you ever go back?
Marlon: **8** Moscow has a very interesting history. You're never bored. (such)
Sure. _____
_____

Consolidation

5 Circle the correct answers.

This week's vacation
What to do in Crete

I went to Crete to try out some water sports. As soon as I arrived, I went to the hotel pool but there were [1] _____ many people that I decided to go to the beach. It was so quiet that I got [2] _____ very quickly. The next day I went back to Heraklion.

I got to the beach early and decided to go snorkelling. It was only eight o'clock but there was [3] _____ long line for snorkels that I left. I wanted to go scuba diving, but the course cost so [4] _____ that I couldn't afford it.

Windsurfing looked easy but was actually difficult. I spent so [5] _____ time in the water that I soon got [6] _____ . Waterskiing was worse. I was [7] _____ bad waterskier that the instructor suggested I try something else! I left the beach [8] _____ quickly that I forgot my clothes! I had to go back for them. I was so [9] _____ about everything that I spent the rest of the day in my hotel room.

On my last day, I tried paragliding. This was the best thing I did. I had [10] _____ awesome time that I couldn't stop smiling. It was [11] _____ amazing to look down on the beach that I spent all day doing it. I recommend it to anyone and Crete is [12] _____ beautiful island that I can't think of anything better than paragliding there.

1 a) so   b) such a   c) such
2 a) thrilled   b) bored   c) ashamed
3 a) such a   b) such   c) so
4 a) much   b) more   c) many
5 a) a lot   b) many   c) much
6 a) tired   b) proud   c) cheerful
7 a) such   b) so   c) such a
8 a) so   b) so many   c) so much
9 a) calm   b) embarrassed   c) amused
10 a) so much   b) such an   c) so
11 a) so   b) such a   c) such
12 a) such   b) so   c) such a

Phrases

1 ★ Complete the conversation with words from the box.

> • Watch out for • That was close • You know

Jed: Hi, Brad! What are you doing here? You don't usually take the train.

Brad: Oh, hi, Jed. I've just finished my tests. I'm going to meet some friends.

Jed: How were your tests?

Brad: They were OK, thanks. Math was really difficult,

1 _____, I don't think I did very well.

Jed: I guess you'll find out in the summer.

Brad: Yeah. Anyway, let's talk about something else. Have you seen my new phone?

Jed: Wow! It's amazing. Oh, no, you dropped it!

2 _____ that train, Brad! Don't try to pick it up now.

Brad: Phew, got it! **3** _____!
       I thought it had fallen onto the track.

Jed: Well let's go. Don't drop your phone again!

Grammar: *used to/be used to/get used to*

2 ★ Complete the sentences with the verbs in parentheses and the correct form of *used to*.

1 David Beckham *used to play* (play) for Manchester United.

2 He *didn't use to be* (not be) a world famous soccer player.

3 Barack Obama _____ (study) at Harvard.

4 He _____ (not live) in Washington.

5 Kate Winslet _____ (have) red hair.

6 She _____ (not have) blond hair.

7 Carla Bruni _____ (work) as a model.

8 She _____ (not be) the French president's wife.

3 ★★ **Look at the magazine article. Complete the interviewer's questions and Sting's answers with *used to*, *be used to*, or *get used to*.**

Sting answers your questions

1 Interviewer: what / you / do / ?
Sting: be / teacher
Interviewer: *What did you use to do?*
Sting: *I used to be a teacher.*
2 Interviewer: Your stage name is Sting. what / your name / use / be / ?
Sting: Gordon Sumner
Interviewer: _____
Sting: _____
3 Interviewer: Why are you called Sting?
Sting: use / wear a black and yellow sweater
Sting: Because _____
_____ so I looked like a bee!
4 Interviewer: Were you always a solo singer?
Sting: (no / be / in a band called The Police)
Sting: _____
5 Interviewer: how long / take you / get used / sing / alone?
Sting: get used to it / very quickly
Interviewer: _____
Sting: _____

Use your English: Ask for and give explanations

4 ★ **Circle the correct answers.**

Tim: Do you want some Marmite?

Alex: What 1 *is* / *be* / *are* Marmite?

Tim: It's 2 *something* / *somewhere* / *someone* that you put on toast for breakfast.

Alex: I've never 3 *known* / *heard* / *thought* of it before.

Tim: It's great!

Nathan: Can I have a peanut butter and jelly sandwich?

Rosy: What do you 4 *know* / *think* / *mean* by jelly? I eat jelly with ice cream!

Nathan: Oh, no, sorry. It's a 5 *kind* / *taste* / *look* of jam. I like strawberry best.

Rosy: Peanut butter and strawberry jam? It 6 *means* / *sounds* / *makes* disgusting!

Jason: Oh wow! I don't believe it. Look, Dr. Pepper.

Sam: I have no 7 *thought* / *idea* / *knowledge* what Dr. Pepper is.

Jason: It's the best drink in the world. It 8 *sounds* / *means* / *tastes* like cherry cola but different.

Sam: It sounds 9 *strange* / *strangely* / *stranger* but I'll try some.

Consolidation

5 Complete the conversation with phrases from the box.

- ~~get used to being~~ • get used to eating
- I'm used to getting up • I'm used to spending
- It means that • It's a kind of • used to go
- not used to eating • What is • You know

Teresa: Diane, why are you awake? It's seven o'clock in the morning.

Diane: I still can't 1 *get used to being* on vacation. 2 _____ at six o'clock for school.

Teresa: Relax! Breakfast isn't until nine o'clock. What are you going to do?

Diane: Don't worry. 3 _____ time alone. I might go for a walk on the beach.

Teresa: Well, I'm going back to bed. I feel sick.

Diane: You're 4 _____ so much. The food here is so amazing!

Teresa: I know. We always 5 _____ to Cancun for our vacations. We had ceviche for dinner nearly every day.

Diane: 6 _____ ceviche?

Teresa: 7 _____ seafood dish. It's delicious and not too filling. Not like the pizzas here. They're so big!

Diane: 8 _____, this is going to sound strange, but I can't 9 _____ real Italian pizzas. They're so thin!

Teresa: That's good, though. 10 _____ you taste the topping, not just the bread.

Will I be able to touch a spider?

Vocabulary: Phrasal verbs with *in*

1 ★ Match the phrasal verbs (1–7) with the definitions (a–g).

1 break in	a) to feel a part of a group, the same as everyone else
2 fit in	b) to give a piece of homework to a teacher
3 give in	c) to become fully understood
4 hand in	d) to admit that you have lost
5 move in	e) to sleep in a hotel room for a time, for example for a vacation
6 sink in	f) to get into a house or other building in order to steal from it
7 stay in	g) to start living in a new home

2 ★★ Complete the e-mail with the correct form of the phrasal verbs (1–7) from Exercise 1.

From:	Jack
To:	Nick

Hi Nick,

Sorry I haven't written for so long. We've finally ¹ _moved in_ to our new house. I can't believe it! It still hasn't ² _____ yet. The house wasn't ready on time, so we had to ³ _____ a hotel for two weeks. It was really expensive!

I don't know if I told you, but my mom and dad decided to move here after burglars ⁴ _____ to our old house three times in a month. They really wanted to stay in Seattle but ⁵ _____ after the third time. The town where we live now is much safer, but we're different from the other people here. I think it's going to take a long time for us to ⁶ _____ with the locals. How long did it take you to get used to your new house when you left Seattle?

Anyway, I have to go. I have a project that I have to ⁷ _____ on Monday.

Hope you're OK. Keep in touch. I hope some of the other people from our old class write. Do they write to you?

Jack

Grammar: *be able to*

3 ★ Complete the sentences with words from the box.

• able • be • been • to • were • weren't • will • ~~won't~~

1 I _won't_ be able to go to your party next week.

2 _____ you be able to buy some milk when you go out?

3 I'm sorry but we _____ able to find out what was wrong with your laptop.

4 When will I _____ able to meet your new boyfriend?

5 You'll be able _____ see the board when you get your glasses.

6 _____ you able to stay awake until the end of the movie last night?

7 How many of your friends were _____ to come to your party?

8 I've never _____ able to understand Physics.

4 ★★ Rewrite the words in parentheses with the correct form of *be able to*.

David Blaine, the American magician, is sometimes called The Modern Houdini, but he ¹ *has been able to do* (has managed to do) things that Houdini never could. In 1999, he lived in a box under water for seven days. It was so small that he ² _____ (couldn't move), and he only had a few spoonfuls of water a day to drink. Houdini had wanted to do a similar trick but he ³ _____ (couldn't) because he died before he got the chance.

The next year, Blaine ⁴ _____ (managed to do) something even more incredible. He survived for sixty-three hours in a block of ice. When workers cut open the ice, Blaine was immediately taken to the hospital. The doctors ⁵ _____ (managed to save) him, but Blaine ⁶ _____ (couldn't walk) for a month.

Most of Blaine's tricks have been done in the U.S., but people in other countries ⁷ _____ (have also managed to see) him.

Blaine knows he has to think of new ideas, even more exciting than before, to keep people interested in him but how ⁸ _____ (will he manage to do) this and stay alive? I'm sure we'll find out soon!

Consolidation

5 **Rearrange the words in parentheses and complete the phrasal verbs.**

1 A: *Will we be able to* (will / we / able) m<u>ove</u> in to our new house over the weekend?

  B: *No, you won't. My men won't be able to finish* (no / my men / not / able / finish) the roof until next week.

2 A: _____ (How / the burglars / able) b_____ in last night? We locked the doors.

  B: _____ (Burglars / always / able) find a way in. One burglar got into the police station last week. He stole our TV.

3 A: Did you h_____ in your math homework?

  B: No. I didn't do it. I _____ _____ (never / be / able) to understand math. I _____ (not able / understand) it last year and I _____ _____ (not able / understand) it next year. I'm glad we don't have any math tests.

  A: . . . Uh, we have a math test tomorrow.

Extra challenge!

6 ★★★ **Complete the sentences so that they are true for you.**

1 When I was ten, I was able to _____

_____.

2 I wish I was able to _____

_____.

3 Next year, I'm sure I'll be able to _____

_____.

4 I've never been able to _____

_____.

5 I never thought I'd be able to _____

_____.

6 If I was able to _____,

  I would _____.

INTEGRATED CONSOLIDATION SKILLS

Charity work

Read

1 ★ Read four news stories and match the celebrities (1–4) with what they did for charity (a–d).

1 Cheryl Cole   a) organized a surfing competition and offered surf lessons.

2 Jennifer Lopez   b) autographed bags for an auction.

3 Rob Machado   c) climbed Mount Kilimanjaro.

4 Jessica Alba   d) took part in a triathlon.

1
Cheryl Cole, singer and wife of soccer player, Ashley Cole, was one of nine celebrities who reached the top of Mount Kilimanjaro yesterday. They climbed the mountain in order to raise money to buy mosquito nets for Tanzania. These will help stop the disease malaria. The climb took five days altogether and the celebrities suffered from back pain and altitude sickness. They left the last camp just after midnight so that they were able to reach the top in time to see the sun rise.

2
Jennifer Lopez has helped to raise $127,000. The money will be given to a children's hospital in Los Angeles. Jennifer and other celebrities took part in a sponsored triathlon. The three events were a one-kilometer swim, a twenty-five-kilometer bike ride and a six-kilometer run. Jennifer's time was two hours and twenty-three minutes. Speaking to reporters, Jennifer said that she was delighted to have finished but hadn't realized how difficult the swimming part would be.

3 Surfers and celebrities in Los Angeles have been raising money for a charity called "Save our Surf." The money raised will be used to keep the ocean clean and help sealife. They raised the money by holding a surfing competition. Champion surfer, Rob Machado, also offered surfing lessons. People had to bid for these and the money went to the charity. Rob Machado was given a special award for all his work for the charity.

4
Jessica Alba has been giving her support to Earth Day. She is one of eight celebrities who have been signing their names on bags which people can then bid for in an online auction. The bags are made of natural cotton with a design by a graffiti artist from Paris. We don't know yet how much money Jessica's bags have raised but we do know that, for every $1 raised, the organization will plant a tree.

Learning strategy: Dictionary skills (3)
Remember! Many words have more than one meaning. Look at the context of the word in the text and the part of speech. Then look in the dictionary and find the meaning that matches the context.

New words and phrases

2 ★★ Look at the new words. Choose the correct meaning in the context of the article.

1 suffered

a) (verb) experienced something unpleasant, such as an illness

b) (verb) became worse

2 sponsored

  a) (verb) the past tense form of the verb to *sponsor*; to give money to a sports team, etc. in return for them advertising your products

  b) (adjective) describing an event which is held to raise money for charity

3 award

  a) (noun) a prize for doing something special

  b) (verb) to give someone a prize for doing something special

4 signing

  a) (noun) a special event at which a famous person signs their book, CD, etc., for fans

  b) (verb) the continuous form of the verb to *sign*; to write your name on something

5 auction

  a) (noun) an event at which things are sold to the person who offers the most money

  b) (verb) to sell at an auction

Comprehension

3 ★★ Read the texts again and write what the numbers refer to.

1 9 *Nine celebrities climbed Mount Kilimanjaro.*

2 5 _____

3 127,000 _____

_____

4 1 _____

Listen

4 ★ 🎧 9 Match the students (1–4) with the ideas for raising money (a–f). There are two extra ideas.

Student 1   a) holding a sponsored dance

Student 2   b) selling things at an auction

Student 3   c) making things and selling them

Student 4   d) having a sports competition

              e) selling tickets to a party

              f) face-painting

5 ★★ Circle the correct answers.

1 Student 1 thinks sponsored dances _____.

  a) raise more money than sponsored walks or swims

  b) are more tiring than sponsored walks or swims

  c) are more fun than sponsored walks or swims

2 Student 2 suggests that if you want to organize a party you need _____.

  a) to pay for a DJ   b) to find sponsors

  c) to find people who will help you for nothing

3 Student 3 thinks face-painting is something that _____.

  a) children like   b) children can do

  c) is fun to do on a sunny day

4 One thing that happened at the auction was that _____.

  a) Student 4 bought things she didn't want

  b) other people bought things she didn't want any more

  c) people spent a lot of time organizing the event

Write

6 ★★ Look at the ad. On a separate sheet of paper, write a formal letter applying for a volunteer job at the sports camp. Use the Writing bank on page 147 of your Student Book to help you.

☆ U.S. Summer Sports Camp ☆

Volunteers needed

We need young people ages fifteen to twenty to help at our summer sports camps. You need to be
* in good shape * imaginative * friendly
* hard-working * enthusiastic
* good with children (ages six to twelve)

Responsibilities

* Organize sports events and train the children
* Help to organize afternoon and evening social events for children
* Help all children get involved and enjoy their time at the camp

Have you had it checked?

Vocabulary: Parts of a bike

1 ★ Look at the pictures and complete the crossword puzzle. Then find the hidden words.

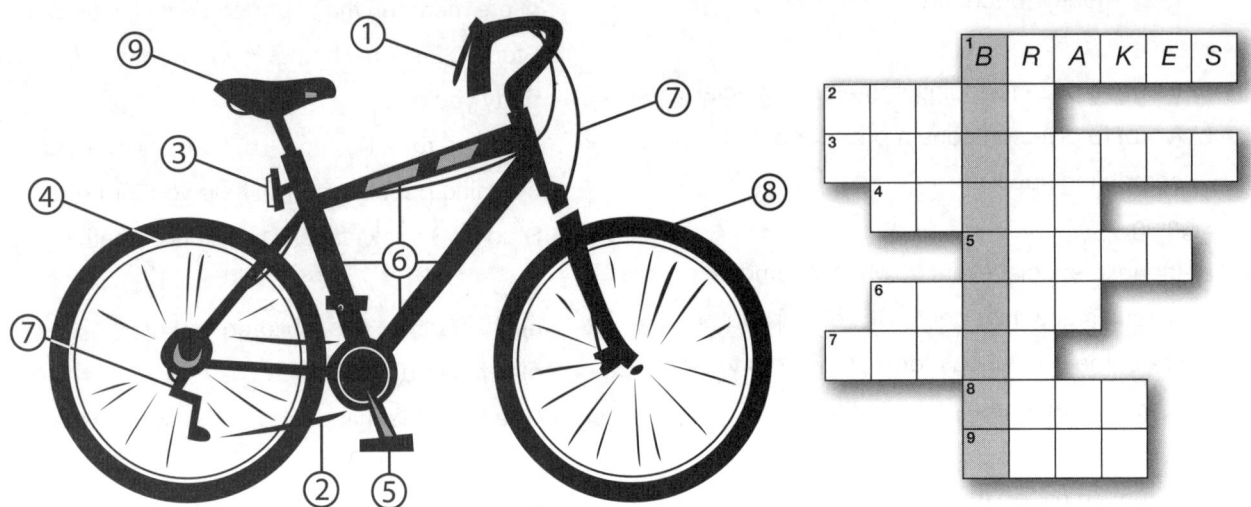

Phrases

2 ★ Match the questions (1–3) to the responses (a–c).

1 Have you seen Jacob's new phone?

2 Does this laptop work?

3 Hey, do you want to buy my bike?

a) Yes, it's in pretty good shape, despite the scratches on the screen.

b) You're kidding. It's a complete wreck and the tires are flat.

c) Yes, but it's not exactly new, is it? It was his brother's.

Grammar: Causative *have*

3 ★ Complete the sentences with the correct form of the verbs in parentheses.

The busy life of Daphne Forbes-Smythe

1 At eight o'clock she always ___*has*___ (have) her breakfast ___*brought*___ (bring) to her bedroom.

2 After breakfast yesterday, she _____ (have) her nails _____ (do).

3 At 10:00 A.M. every day, she _____ (have) her e-mails _____ (write) for her.

4 At the moment, she _____ (have) her photograph _____ (take).

5 Later today, she is going _____ (have) a special pizza _____ (make) for her lunch.

4 ★★ Write sentences with causative *have*.

1 I / take passport photo / yesterday

I had my passport photo taken yesterday.

2 I need / mend pants / before tomorrow

_____

3 I'm going / clean computer / tomorrow

_____

4 Jess / pierce ears / never

_____

5 Jess / cut hair / today

_____

6 My parents / wash windows / yesterday

_____

Use your English: Describe and deal with problems

5 ★ Complete the chat with words from the box.

> • change • doesn't • fix • makes • nothing
> • problem • sure • think • wrong

```
000
← · → · ℮ ⊗ ⌂ [                    ]
```

Computer problems/general

A forum to give and receive computer help
Note: We are not responsible for any advice given here. You should contact an expert if you are unsure.
Nick: I have a ¹ *problem* with my computer. Can anyone out there help?
Laughing boy: Well, maybe. What's ² _____ with it?
Nick: I'm trying to burn some DVDs but the DVD drive ³ _____ work very well ☹. It ⁴ _____ a strange noise when I put a DVD in.
Iceman: You should change it.
Nick: I'm not ⁵ _____ I can do that.
Laughing boy: Be brave! It's not difficult. ☺
Iceman: No, don't listen to him. Take it to a store.
Nick: Do you ⁶ _____ they could ⁷ _____ the problem for me?
Iceman: It depends on the problem. If there's ⁸ _____ they can do, they'll ⁹ _____ the drive for you. A new one will cost about $40.

Consolidation

6 Write sentences. Unscramble the letters in parentheses to make bike parts. Change the underlined words to the causative *have* form.

1 The (cabk igtlh) didn't work so <u>someone replaced it</u>.

The *back light* didn't work so *I had it replaced* .

2 The front (helwe) wobbled <u>but no one has changed it</u> yet.

The front *wheel* wobbled but I *haven't had it changed* yet.

3 The (reasg) were perfect so <u>no one needed to look at them</u>.

The _____ were perfect so I _____

_____ .

4 The (sarkbe) were sticking so <u>someone checked them</u>.

The _____ were sticking so I _____

_____ .

5 The (aset) was too low so <u>someone had to raise it</u>.

The _____ was too low so I _____

_____ .

6 The (ahnci) is dirty but <u>no one cleaned it</u>. I can do that myself.

The _____ is dirty but I _____

_____ . I can do that myself.

7 The (efarm) is a horrible color. <u>I'm going to ask someone to repaint it</u>.

The _____ is a horrible color. I _____

_____ .

8 Oh, no! Now the (edlpsa) and (anhsabrdel) are loose. I don't think <u>I'll ask anyone to fix them</u>. I think I'll get a new bike!

Now the _____ and _____ are loose.

I don't think _____

_____ .

I think I'll get a new bike!

Grammar: Clauses of purpose: *to, in order (not) to, so that*

1 ★ Match the beginnings (1–6) to the endings (a–f).

1 I study French
2 I went to the club
3 We often go to a restaurant
4 I have a weekend job
5 I called my friend
6 I wanted to see my teacher

a) to see what the new DJ was like.
b) to ask if she wanted to meet.
c) so that I can understand my friend in Nice.
d) so that Dad can eat steak.
e) in order to ask about the homework he gave us.
f) so that I can save some money for the summer.

2 ★★ Complete the sentences with *in order to, in order (not) to,* or *so that*.

Things you need to know

1 Lights must be turned off at 10 P.M. *in order not to* disturb people who want to sleep.

2 Rooms are locked from 10 A.M. to 3 P.M. _____ we can clean them.

3 We ask you not to eat in the rooms _____ keep them as clean as possible.

4 Please leave money in the office _____ lose it.

3 ★★ Complete the sentences with clauses of purpose. Put the verbs in the correct form.

Alex agrees to join MI6 . . .

1 Jack / not get into trouble
so that Jack doesn't get
into trouble .

2 help / Jack stay out of trouble
in order to help Jack stay
out of trouble .

Frodo put on the One Ring . . .

5 no one / could see him

_____
_____ .

6 hide / from Boromir

_____
_____ .

Humans travel to Pandora . . .

3 they / can get a valuable mineral

_____
_____ .

4 take / "unobtanium" and bring it to Earth

_____
_____ .

The animals repaired the plane . . .

7 could / get home again

_____
_____ .

8 leave / Madagascar

_____
_____ .

Vocabulary: Adjective suffixes with -ful, -y, -ous, -ive, -al

4 ★ Use the words from the box to write adjectives with the endings given.

> • ambition • danger • effect • imagine • music
> • ~~profession~~ • salt • sun • use • wonder

-al: _professional_ , _____

-ful: _____ , _____

-ive: _____ , _____

-ous: _____ , _____

-y: _____ , _____

5 ★★ Complete the e-mail with the adjective form of the words in parentheses.

To: Kristina
From: Bradley
Attachments: cover 1.jpg cover 2.jpg

Dear Kristina,

Several children sent us ideas for the cover of our new children's magazine. It was difficult to choose a winner so I chose two! They are attached. Some of the ideas looked very [1] _professional_ (profession) with [2] _____ (beauty) artwork. However, we didn't choose them. Although they were very [3] _____ (attract), we were a bit [4] _____ (suspicion) that the children hadn't actually designed them themselves.

The two I've attached are very different from each other. The first is a [5] _____ (wonder) and very [6] _____ (imagine) picture. I think you'll like it. The second is a [7] _____ (mystery) entry. It's a very [8] _____ (origin) design but we have no idea who sent it in. There's a name and phone number on it. We called but the person said that they hadn't entered our competition!

The competition has been a huge success. It has been a very [9] _____ (use) way to find out about our readers and an [10] _____ (effect) way to design our first cover, or two!

Bradley

Consolidation

6 Complete the text with the correct form of the words in parentheses and *so that* or *in order to*.

Good advice

Your tips about ANYTHING!

Don't buy chips! They make them [1] _salty_ (salt) [2] _____ make you [3] _____ (thirst)! Then you spend money on drinks. The same company makes the chips and the drinks. They just want more of your money!

Be careful on [4] _____ (sun) days! The sun is [5] _____ (danger). You should put on strong sunscreen [6] _____ you don't get burned.
(Tami, age 13)

Don't go to see the movie *Dance and Sing*! The reviews said it was [7] _____ (wonder) but it was awful! I was [8] _____ (suspicion) when I saw who was in it. I was right. They couldn't dance and they couldn't sing! I think they called it *Dance and Sing* [9] _____ people would think it was like *High School Musical*. **(Emma, age 15)**

Don't have your photo taken at Fred's Studio. He isn't a [10] _____ (profession) photographer. He didn't take the [11] _____ (attract) photos outside his studio. They are there [12] _____ make people think that he can take good photos, but he can't!
(Lou, age 14)

It sounds like a police siren.

Vocabulary: Adjectives of texture and shape

1 ★ Circle the correct answers.

1 A _____ photograph
   (a) triangular   b) round
   c) square

2 A _____ bed
   a) curved   b) straight
   c) round

3 A _____ table
   a) round   b) square
   c) rectangular

4 A _____ book
   a) curved   b) thick
   c) thin

5 A _____ -shaped
   notebook
   a) square   b) triangular
   c) star

6 A _____ line
   a) round   b) straight
   c) curved

2 ★★ Complete the conversations.

1 **Sally:** The skin on my hands is really rough.

  Anne: This cream will make them _____soft_____.

2 **Allie:** Aahh. This floor is really s_____.
   I nearly fell.

  Delia: Oh, sorry. I just washed it.

3 **Mike:** What's wrong?

  Tom: I didn't realize that plant had p_____
   leaves. Look, there's blood on my finger.

4 **Mom:** What are you doing?

  Dad: I'm putting up this shelf.

  Mom: But the wood's all rough. You should make
   it nice and s_____ before you put
   it up.

5 **Jess:** Why do you like rabbits?

  Chloe: I like their f_____ little tails!

Grammar: *look, seem, sound, feel, taste, smell* + adjective /*like*/*as if*

3 ★ Circle the correct answers.

Ryan: Hi, Grace. It's Ryan.

Grace: Oh. Your voice 1 *sounds* / *looks* / *feels* funny.

Ryan: I have a cold.

Aaron: Hi, Chris. Are you OK?

Chris: Yes, why?

Aaron: You 2 *feel* / *look* / *taste* worried.

Chris: Oh, it's these tests.

Jason: What's on this pizza?

Ellen: Tomatoes, chicken, and onions. Why?

Jason: It 3 *sounds* / *feels* / *tastes* strange.

Ellen: Yuck! It 4 *sounds* / *seems* / *smells* strange, too!

Kelly: What did you think of the new girl?

Mia: I don't know. I didn't speak to her but she
   5 *seemed* / *sounded* / *felt* nice.

Kelly: She's a little quiet, though.

Mia: She probably 6 *looked* / *felt* / *sounded*
   nervous on her first day at the school.

4 ★★ Complete the sentences with the correct form of the word and any other words necessary.

1 LOOK

Steve _____*looks*_____ terrible.

He ___*looks as if*___ he hasn't slept for a week.

He ___*looks like*___ my dad when he works late.

2 SOUND

Jackie _____ an old woman.

She _____ she has a cold.

She _____ strange.

3 SMELL

This chicken _____ (not) good.

It _____ (not) chicken should.

It _____ it's been left in the sun for a few days.

4 FEEL

This shirt _____ (not) silk.

It _____ it's been washed in cheap detergent.

It _____ (not) smooth.

Consolidation

5 Look at the pictures and complete the sentences.

①  It 👀 ___*looks*___ like silk but it

doesn't 🤚 ___*feel*___ like

silk. Silk is ___*soft*___ not rough.

② 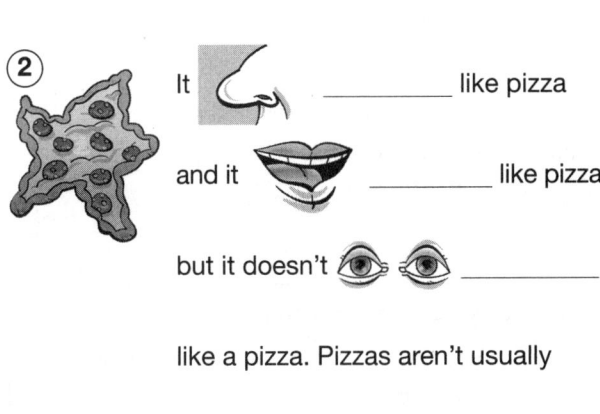 It 👃 _____ like pizza

and it 👄 _____ like pizza

but it doesn't 👀 _____

like a pizza. Pizzas aren't usually

s_____-shaped!

③ **Go away!** He 👀 👀 _____ friendly

but he doesn't 👂 _____ very friendly.

④ **Ooh, baby I love you.** They 👂 _____ like a

rock group but they don't 👀 👀

_____ like a rock group!

⑤ This t_____ chair doesn't

👀 👀 _____ very

comfortable but this cushion

🤚 _____ nice and soft.

Extra challenge!

6 ★★★ Complete the sentences and then circle the correct answers.

1 It looks ___*like*___ a snake but it swims in the sea.
a) a worm (b) an eel) c) a lizard

2 They sound _____ they are laughing.
a) hyenas b) camels c) llamas

3 It feels _____ silk but it is man-made.
a) wool b) cotton c) rayon

4 Some people say they sound _____ the Beatles.
a) Oasis b) U2 c) Take That

5 In the movie *Benjamin Button* he looks _____ he's really old.
a) George Clooney b) Johnny Depp c) Brad Pitt

INTEGRATED
CONSOLIDATION
SKILLS

Work experience

Read

1 ★ Match the headings (1–5) to the ads (A–E).

1 I need people to help me

2 Learn about working in a large store

3 A chance to learn office skills

4 Social organizers for foreign students

5 Have fun and learn interesting facts

A 3
Are you fifteen to eighteen years old?
We can offer you a great experience this summer. Something that will look good on your resume and allow you to work with some great people in a modern, friendly office. You will learn how to type, file, photocopy, take messages, and write reports. We will pay you a small salary.

B
Do you like working outside?
Why not help out in your local zoo this summer? We need volunteers to feed the animals, clean the cages, and keep the zoo looking neat. It's fun and you'll learn a lot about how animals live and how we look after them. No pay but meals are provided.

C
Summer school requires volunteers.
You will organize evening social events for the students. You will live at the summer camp and we offer free meals plus a small amount of pocket money. Great experience for anyone thinking about becoming a language teacher when they leave school.

D
Summer workers needed.
As part of our management training program, you will work in all departments of the store. Duties will include customer service, stocktaking, ordering, and shelf filling. Good workers may be offered sponsorship through college and a job in one of our stores after school.

E
Researchers required by busy politician.
I'm looking for two or three young people to help out by researching articles on the Internet, correcting facts and spelling mistakes in my blog, and updating my Web pages. Some travel may be necessary. I will pay for all transportation, hotels, and food.

Comprehension

2 ★★ Match the questions (1–10) with the correct job ads (A–E).

Which job . . .

1 pays some money to people who work there in the summer? A C

2 asks for people of a certain age?

3 doesn't mention food?

4 might offer work in the future?

5 could be useful for people who like teaching?

6 could involve travel?

7 needs someone to use a computer?

8 helps people to learn about animals?

9 needs people to live and work in the same place?

10 means that you will work outside all the time?

Listen

Learning strategy: Listen for linking phrases

Remember! When you hear a linking phrase such as *for example*, *because of this*, or *as a result*, you can predict the kind of information you will hear.

3a ★ Look at the linking phrases. Before you listen, guess which information you are likely to hear.

1 The job seems to offer the opportunity to gain a wide range of experience, *for example* . . .
You expect to hear . . .
a) things like filing, photocopying, and typing.
b) things like money, free meals, and travel costs.
c) things like work hours, qualifications, and pay.

2 I worked in a store on Saturdays and, *as a result of that* . . .
You expect to hear . . .
a) the types of work he did on Saturdays.
b) what he did on a Saturday evening.
c) how his work in the store changed him in some way.

3 He (the owner of the store where I worked) wasn't very happy with me. *Because of that* . . .
You expect to hear . . .
a) the reasons why the owner wasn't happy.
b) what the owner did when the speaker asked for his job back.
c) what kind of job the speaker used to do.

b ★ 🎧10 Now listen to an interview for summer work and check your answers to Exercise 3a.

4 ★★ Listen again and circle the correct answers.

1 Luke is ____.
a) in 10th grade   b) in a band
c) a member of the school drama club

2 Luke is interested in the job because ____.
a) of the money offered
b) of the things he will learn
c) he likes working in offices

3 Luke has ____.
a) never worked before
b) worked in an office before
c) worked before but not in an office

4 Luke stopped working ____.
a) in April
b) after his final exams
c) because the store owner was angry with him

5 The owner of the store was angry because ____.
a) no one else wanted to work for him
b) Luke was a bad worker
c) Luke wanted to work in an office

6 Luke ____.
a) is upset that he can't work in a store
b) needs to earn more money
c) would prefer to work in the office than a store

Write

5 ★ Complete the letter with words from the box.

> • example • interested • store • summer
> • sure • that

Dear Sam,

I heard from your mother that you are looking for a 1 _____ job. I know a few people in business and I'm 2 _____ that I could help. Let me know what kind of work you want (office, 3 _____, outdoors, restaurant, summer school) and what you want from it, for 4 _____, money, exciting experiences, etc.

Also, I know I haven't seen you for a long time so tell me about yourself. What are you 5 _____ in? That's the kind of thing I need to know so 6 _____ I can help you find the best job.

All the best,

Uncle John

6 ★★ On a separate sheet of paper, write a letter to your uncle telling him about yourself and what kind of work you are interested in.

73

He shouldn't have left it there.

Phrases

1 ★ Complete the phrases.

1 **Matt:** Do you think anyone will buy my computer?

   Simon: What? T_hat_____ o_____ thing? I don't think so!

2 **Kylie:** My parents say that I have to be home by 10 P.M.

   Beth: W_____ a d_____! Malcolm's parties are always so good.

3 **Natalie:** Where's Mrs. Taylor? She should be here by now.

   Cheryl: W_____ a m_____. I'll see if she's in the staff room.

Grammar: *should have/ought to have*

2 ★ Complete the blog with the correct form of the verbs in parentheses.

▽ | _ ▬ ✕

Saturday, November 10

What a terrible week at school! I wish I could go back and change it. What did I do wrong? Here's my confession!

- Sunday: I shouldn't **1** _have stayed_ (stay) up so late. I was *so* tired on Monday!
- Monday: I ought **2** _____ (study) more for my test. I did *really* badly!
- Tuesday: I shouldn't **3** _____ (believe) Melanie's gossip about Susie.
- Wednesday: I ought not **4** _____ (turn on) my phone in English. The teacher was *really* angry when it rang!
- Thursday: I should **5** _____ (go) straight home after school. Mom was so worried that now she's going to pick me up every day.
- Friday: I ought **6** _____ (remember) my books.
- Friday: I shouldn't **7** _____ (write) notes to Maria during the math test. The teacher thought I was cheating.

3 ★★ Complete the e-mail with the positive or negative form of *should* (s) or *ought to* (o) and the correct form of the verbs from the box.

- allow • ask • ~~buy~~ • leave • look • make
- ~~plan~~ • take • wear

From:	Lizzie
≡▼ To:	Rhani

Hi Rhani,

Thanks for the e-mail! Don't worry! It wasn't your fault that the weekend was a disaster.

We [1](s) _should have planned_ everything more carefully. We definitely [2](o) _ought to have bought_ the bus tickets in advance. I didn't know the buses were so busy. The driver [3](o) _____ us to stand. He [4](s) _____ us wait for two hours until the next bus arrived.

We [5](s) _____ at some websites before we left. It wasn't fun trying to find somewhere to stay in the rain!

The walk on Sunday was nice but, yes, you were right again! We [6](o) _____ a map with us and we [7](s) _____ more comfortable shoes, too—my feet were so sore!

I'm sorry about the money, too. I [8](s) _____ it lying on the bed for everyone to see. I'm sure someone saw it there and stole it. It wasn't all bad though, was it? We met Mike and Tom. They were really nice and very funny! We [9](s) _____ them for their e-mail addresses! Still, maybe we can look them up on Facebook!

Anyway, I have to go now and do some homework! See you soon!

Love,

Lizzie

Use your English: Apologize for past mistakes

4 ★ Complete the conversations with words and phrases from the box.

- all right • At least • back very late
- Look • so late • so sorry • That's OK
- ~~waiting~~ • you been

Conversation 1

Nathan: I've been **1** _waiting_ for you for a long time. Why are you **2** _____?

Elizabeth: I'm **3** _____. I had to wait for my mom to come home.

Nathan: That's **4** _____. The movie hasn't started yet.

Conversation 2

Mrs. Hird: You're **5** _____ from school. Where have **6** _____?

Kelly: I'm sorry. We had extra practice for the school play and I didn't have my phone with me.

Mrs. Hird: **7** _____.
8 _____ you're back home safely.

Conversation 3

Mr. Grayson: **9** _____ at your homework! What happened to it?

Peter: I'm really sorry. My little brother spilled his juice all over it.

Mr. Grayson: OK. Do it again tonight and give it to me tomorrow.

Consolidation

5 Complete the online messages with one word in each blank.

New application—the apology board

Apologize to others and accept their apologies to you!

Mira: **1** _Sorry_ I can't come to your party tonight. I should **2** _____ called you earlier. My sister needs a babysitter.

Anna: **3** _____ a drag! Hope you can make it next time!

Tom: I ought **4** _____ to have said those things about your new haircut. Sorry!

Anna: That's **5** _____ right. I don't really like it, either.

Nikki: Sorry I haven't e-mailed for so long. I've been studying for my exams! I ought **6** _____ have done a lot more work!

Anna: No problem. Get in touch after your exams are done

Jake: Hi! I'm sorry about not waiting for you outside the theater last night, but it was really cold.

Anna: **7** _____ at least you got to see the beginning of the movie . I **8** _____ have called you. Was it a good movie?

Jake: It was OK but a bit difficult to understand. I **9** _____ to have read the reviews before I went.

Vocabulary: Phrasal verbs with *away*

1 ★ Circle the correct verbs.

1 The thief ____ away and the police couldn't stop him.

   a) threw   (b) ran)   c) gave

2 Mr. Smith ____ the tickets away accidentally.

   a) gave   b) put   c) threw

3 Jessica didn't like the scary parts so she ____ away from the TV.

   a) passed   b) looked   c) put

4 Toby ____ his old toys away to the thrift shop.

   a) gave   b) put   c) threw

5 The students of Class 5C are ____ their books away.

   a) throwing   b) passing   c) putting

6 The fish ____ away.

   a) got   b) threw   c) gave

Grammar: *must/can't/might/could* for deductions in the present

2 ★ Match the sentences (1–9) with the correct reasons (a–i).

1 He must be the new teacher.

2 He can't be the new teacher.

3 He might be the new teacher.

a) I think we're getting one today.

b) I saw him in the teachers' room.

c) He's too young.

4 There can't be a monster in here.

5 There might be a monster in here.

6 There must be a monster in here.

d) Anything's possible!

e) So many people have seen it.

f) Monsters don't exist.

7 Aliens can't really exist.

8 Aliens must exist.

9 Aliens might exist.

g) There are so many planets.

h) I mean, why not?

i) It's just impossible.

3 ★★ Complete the conversation. Write *must*, *can't*, *might*, or *could*, and a verb from the box in each blank.

> • ~~be~~ • be • be • find • have • know
> • love • think

Rose: Hi Dan! What are you doing looking in the trash? The concert starts in an hour.

Dan: I'm . . . uh looking for something.

Rose: What are you looking for? It **1** _must be_ important for you to be doing it now. I thought you would be ready to go.

Dan: Well, I'm not ready because, you see, um, I lost the tickets.

Rose: What! I don't believe you! Well, they **2** _____ in the trash. You're always so careful. Look in your wallet. You **3** _____ them in there.

Dan: I thought of that. I've checked there twice.

Rose: I'll ask your mom. She **4** _____ where they are.

Dan: She doesn't. I asked her earlier. I'm so sorry, Rose. You **5** _____ I'm really stupid!

Rose: Don't worry. I know. I'll look in your school jacket . . . Dan, here they are!

Dan: Hang on! These are for tomorrow's concert.

Rose: Tomorrow? Are you going again, tomorrow? Wow! You **6** _____ Bloc Party.

Dan: I do. They're great. I'm going with my brother tomorrow. Hey! That's it! He **7** _____ today's tickets.

Rose: Great! Where is he? He **8** _____ here somewhere.

Dan: He's upstairs, in his room. Wait here and I'll get the tickets . . .

Consolidation

4 Circle the correct answers.

Martha: Where's the newspaper?

Dad: I **1** *put / gave /* (*threw*) it away so it **2** *might / can't / must* be in the recycling box.

Mom: Your room is very neat!

Donna: I know. I **3** *passed / gave / put* all my things away in the dresser.

Mom: You **4** *might / can't / must* be expecting your friends. You only clean up for them!

Dad: Oh, dear. Look at this. Catherine Tillerton **5** *has got / gone / passed* away.

Sam: Who's Catherine Tillerton?

Dad: She was a movie star. You **6** *must / can't / might* be a real movie fan! She was a Hollywood legend.

Jon: Mom, I can't find my striped shirt.

Mom: Have you looked in your bedroom? It **7** *might / can't / must* be under your bed.

Jon: I've looked everywhere. Anyway, it **8** *must / might / can't* be under my bed or in my bedroom. I cleaned my room last night.

Mom: Oh! Hang on! I just remembered. I **9** *gave / threw / put* it away to a thrift shop last week. It was too small for you.

Jon: No way! Oh mom! I loved that shirt.

Extra challenge!

5 ★★★ Look at the information and answer the questions using *must/can't* or *might/could*.

> *The Bodmin Cat*
>
> *Lots of people have seen it.*
> *No large cats have escaped from zoos.*
> *Some farmers say their sheep have disappeared but no one knows how.*

1 Does the Bodmin cat really exist?

   It must exist because lots of people have seen it .

2 Is it from a zoo?

   _____.

3 What does it eat?

   _____.

Vocabulary: Crime

1 ★ Match the beginnings (1–9) with the correct endings (a–i).

1 Sergeant Henderson arrested _____f_____

2 Jake broke _____

3 Angela has never committed _____

4 Fred was sentenced _____

5 Mrs. Jenkins had to pay _____

6 Dan robbed _____

7 Annie stole _____

8 Rick drew _____

9 Mick mugged _____

a) a crime.

b) graffiti all over the bus stop.

c) a fine.

d) the local bank.

e) to three years in prison.

f) ~~the criminal and took him to the police station.~~

g) $500 from a store.

h) an old lady in the street.

i) into the post office at night.

2 ★ Circle the correct answers.

1 The salesperson accused Diane ___ stealing a chocolate bar.

   (a) of   b) for   c) with

2 The police arrested my mom ____ driving too fast.

   a) with   b) of   c) for

3 Paul was sentenced ____ three months in prison.

   a) for   b) of   c) to

4 The police suspected my dad ____ being a burglar when he climbed through the window!

   a) of   b) with   c) for

5 The police charged Toby ____ vandalizing the bus stop.

   a) for   b) with   c) of

6 In court, Henry was convicted ____ stealing cars.

   a) with   b) of   c) for

Grammar: *must have/can't have/ might have/could have* for deductions in the past

3 ★ Complete the sentences with *must have, can't have, might have,* or *could have,* and the verbs in parentheses.

1 The burglar _____*must have climbed*_____ (climb) through the window.

2 We _____ (close) the window before we went out.

3 He _____ (try) to open the front door first but it was locked.

4 He _____ (have) dirty boots on.

5 He _____ (walk) across the garden. Let's go and see if there are any footprints there.

6 The burglar _____ (hear) a noise and left in a hurry.

7 He _____ (see) the computer. It's still here on the desk.

8 He walked straight to the painting. He

_____ (know) that the money was behind it.

4 ★★ Read the texts and make deductions using the cues and *must have, can't have, might have, or could have*.

The Gardner Museum Mystery

What we know

Thirteen paintings disappeared worth $200 million. The police have never caught the thieves. They are sure that the paintings are now in Europe. They think the criminals sold them secretly. There is no way the criminals still have them because they want the money not the paintings. One theory is that a local group of criminals organized the crime but no one really knows. Whoever it was knew exactly what they were doing. Only very clever criminals could have done what they did.

1 The criminals / sell the paintings

   The criminals must have sold the paintings.

2 The criminals / keep the paintings

   _____

3 A local group of criminals / organize the crime

   _____

4 The criminals / be very clever

   _____

The mystery of Stonehenge

What we know

Approximately 4,000 years ago someone transported these giant stones hundreds of miles. It probably took many years to complete. No one really knows what it was for. One theory is that it was for watching the stars. The only thing we can be sure of is that it was definitely important.

5 Stonehenge / be important

   _____

6 It / be easy to build

   _____

7 People / use it for watching the stars

   _____

8 It / take a long time to complete

   _____

Consolidation

5 Complete sentences 1b–4b with one word in each blank so that they mean the same as sentences 1a–4a.

1a Someone came into my house and stole several things. I guess the front door wasn't locked.

2a Someone stole $100,000 from the bank. The police don't know who did it but one idea is that it was an employee.

3a The police said that Jake had vandalized the mall but he isn't in prison. He just had to pay $100.

4a Mary has never broken the law. She's a sweet old lady. I can't believe that she helped to break into the post office!

1b Someone ___robbed___ my house. I ___must not___ have locked the door.

2b Someone _____ the bank. The police think it _____ have been an employee.

3b The police _____ Jake of vandalizing the mall but he didn't _____ to prison. He had to pay a _____ of $100.

4b Mary has never _____ a crime. She's a sweet old lady. She _____ have helped to break into the post office!

Across cultures

INTEGRATED
CONSOLIDATION
SKILLS

Social customs

Read

1 ★ Read the text quickly. Circle the correct answers.

1 Alice is moving to   a) Egypt. (b) Kenya.) c) Argentina.

2 Steve lives in   a) Egypt. b) Kenya. c) Argentina.

3 Theresa's friend is from   a) Egypt. b) Kenya. c) Argentina.

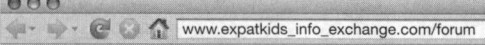

www.expatkids_info_exchange.com/forum

Hi. My family is moving to Kenya for a year. Can anyone give me some guidelines on social customs? *Alice, age 15*

You'll love Kenya, Alice. It's a beautiful country. When you meet people, you usually shake hands. If you're invited to a Kenyan home, you should take cakes, candies, or flowers. Try to remember to give them to your host with your right hand or both hands. You should always wash your hands before you eat. They will probably bring you a bowl and water for this. Try to finish everything on your plate and have fun! *Barack, age 16*

I'm living in Egypt and my Egyptian friend has invited me to dinner at his house. I'm a little nervous. Please help! *Steve, age 14*

I've lived in Egypt for six years and I suggest you take some sweet cakes as a present. At dinner, remember that Egyptians always leave some food on their plate at the end of the main course. That's good if you don't like the food! Even if you do like it, though, you should leave some. After dinner you will get black tea. You shouldn't stay long after this. It means it is time for you to go home. Drink the tea and then say thank you and start to get ready to leave. *Ahmed, age 15*

Can anyone help me? I'm going to dinner at my friend's house. She's Argentinian. I don't want to look rude . . . *Theresa, age 15*

Hi, Theresa. I can help. First, dress nicely. Wear a dress or a skirt and blouse. You shouldn't arrive on time. Come thirty minutes late—really! Argentinians aren't punctual like Americans! Take a small present. You shouldn't start eating until you are invited to do so, and leave a little bit of food on your plate. When you leave, say good-bye to everyone individually. Shake their hands, starting with the oldest. Have a good meal! *Tia, age 15*

New words and phrases

2 ★★ Match the new words or phrases (1–5) with the definitions (a–e).

1 guidelines   a) (noun) the second part of a meal

2 main course   b) (adjective) on time, prompt

3 rude   c) (adverb) separately

4 punctual   d) (adjective) not polite

5 individually   e) (noun) rules or hints for what to do

Comprehension

3 ★★ Read the texts and match the customs to the correct countries. Write K (Kenya), E (Egypt), or A (Argentina).

1 You ought not to finish everything on your plate. `E` `A`

2 You should wear nice clothes to someone's house. ☐

3 Presents should not be given with your left hand. ☐

4 You should shake everyone's hand when you leave. ☐

5 It is easy to know when you should leave. ☐

6 Cakes make a good host present. ☐☐

Listen

4 ★ 🎧 11 Listen to a woman talking to the principal of her son's international school in Japan. Put the stages (a–d) in order. Then match each stage (a–d) to what it means (i–iv).

a) The routine. ☐

b) The vacation. ☐

c) The shock. ☐

d) The worry. ☐

i) Differences between cultures make people depressed and confused.

ii) Returning home causes new problems.

iii) Life in the new country becomes normal.

iv) Everything in the new culture seems exciting and new.

5 ★★ 🎧 11 Listen again and decide whether the sentences are T (true) or F (false).

1 Leo was unhappy when he first moved to Japan. ☐

2 Leo has been in Japan for six months. ☐

3 Leo plays a lot of video games. ☐

4 Leo is going to stay in Japan for one year. ☐

5 Leo's problem is not very common. ☐

6 Leo should be happier soon. ☐

7 The last problem won't affect Leo while he is in Japan. ☐

8 Leo's mother read about culture shock problems before she went to Japan. ☐

Write

> **Writing tip:** *On the other hand, in spite of this, consequently, because of this*
> **Remember!**
> **Contrast:** *If it's somebody older, I usually shake hands.* **On the other hand**, *if it's a good friend, I give them a hug.*
> **Concession:** *Spanish people like to stay up late.* **In spite of this**, *they always get up early for work!*
> **Cause:** *In my country, greetings are quite formal.* **Consequently/Because of this**, *people often think we're unfriendly.*

6 ★ Circle the correct linking phrases.

1 Both my parents work. *On the other hand /* (*In spite of this*), my mom does all the cooking.

2 My grandparents live near us. *On the other hand / Consequently*, we see them almost every day.

3 We all have to do housework every day. *In spite of this / Because of this*, the house always looks messy.

4 We have final exams in January and June. *Because of this / On the other hand*, there's a lot of work to do then.

5 I don't mind sharing a room with my brother. *On the other hand / Because of this*, it's great when he goes out and I have the room to myself.

7 ★★ Imagine a friend from a different country is coming to stay with you on an exchange visit. Think about the social customs and rules in your home and school they might find strange. On a separate sheet of paper, write a letter telling them about these customs. Try to use the linking phrases from Exercise 6.

Dear _____,

I'm really excited about your visit. I'm sure you'll like it here. Before you arrive, I want to tell you a little about my family and home life and also what it's like in our school so that you aren't too surprised . . .

The photos were sold.

Vocabulary: The media

1 ★ Complete the words with one letter in each blank.

1 I have my own b _l_ _o_ _g_ and I write my
   opinions on it every day.

2 N _ _ _ p _ _ _ _ _ are interesting but you
   need a lot of time to read them.

3 My mom loves reading t _ _ l _ _ _
   newspapers because she likes celebrity gossip.

4 I bought the paper when I saw the
   h _ _ d _ _ _ _ _ about Brad Pitt.

5 I read m _ _ a _ _ n _ _ , not newspapers.

6 We have satellite TV and we can get over 100
   different c _ _ n _ e _ _ .

7 Don't worry about missing the radio show. You
   can download the p _ _ c _ _ _ _ .

8 There was a r _ p _ _ _ _ on the news about
   the number of burglaries in our area.

9 The journalist wrote an article about pollution
   but the e _ _ t _ _ didn't want to publish it in
   the newspaper.

Grammar: The passive: simple present, simple past, pesent perfect, past perfect

2 ★ Circle the active or passive form.

Some stars **1**(like) / *are liked* the paparazzi because they
make them feel important. Their photographs **2***publish / are
published* in many magazines and newspapers all over the world.
Photographers **3***often pay / are often paid* lots of money by these
magazines and newspapers. However, celebrities sometimes get
so angry with the paparazzi that they **4***attack / are attacked* them.
Recently, one photographer **5***claimed / was claimed* that Keanu
Reeves had attacked him. He said that he **6***had hurt / had been
hurt* and couldn't work. Keanu Reeves **7***didn't believe / wasn't
believed* him and wanted to show that the photographer was
lying. So, the photographer **8***filmed / was filmed* secretly by a
private detective. The photographer was working and he was still
taking photographs. There was nothing wrong with him! In the
end, Keanu was right after all.

3 ★★ Transform the active sentences into the passive. Use *by* + agent where necessary.

1 My friend wrote this article.

   This article was written by my friend.

2 My friends didn't tell me about the party.

   _____

3 Photographers photographed Brad Pitt as he
   left the restaurant.

   _____

4 Millions of viewers watched the reality show.

   _____

5 Our teacher has given us lots of homework this
   week.

   _____

6 Jack Stevens wrote the graffiti on the subway.

   _____

4 ★★ Complete the text with the correct passive form of the verbs in parentheses.

Where does the word *paparazzi* come from? What does it mean? It ¹*was* first *used* (use) in 1960 in an Italian movie. The movie ² _____ (call) *La Dolce Vita*. One of the characters in the film was a photographer and the character ³ _____ (give) the name Paparazzo by the director Frederico Fellini. In Italian, this means "an annoying noise." It is the sound that ⁴ _____ (make) by a mosquito. Fellini ⁵ _____ (ask) in an interview why he chose that name and he said that he had gone to school with a boy who ⁶ _____ (give) the nickname Paparazzo by his friends. However, Fellini may have gotten the idea from somewhere else. Ennio Flaiano, who worked with Fellini, said that they had found the name in a book which ⁷ _____ (write) long before Fellini's film. Since *La Dolce Vita* ⁸ _____ first _____ (show) in 1960, the word *paparazzo* ⁹ _____ (use) all over the world to describe news photographers.

Consolidation

5 Circle the correct answers.

Adam: Hello Ross.

Ross: Oh, hi, Adam! What are you reading about?

Adam: A new reality show that
1 (*was shown*)/ *showed* / *is shown* last night.

Ross: A reality TV show? I thought newspapers wrote about politics and stuff like that.

Adam: Well, you're half right. Reality TV shows
2 *usually watch* / *are usually watching* /
are usually watched by people who read
3 *magazines* / *headlines* / *tabloids* but this is an interesting article. It wasn't a normal reality show. It was *Big Brother* for children aged eight to eleven.

Ross: You're joking! What **4** *show* / *channel* / *podcast* was that on?

Adam: Channel 4. It says here that it was awful.

Ross: Why? Because nothing happened?

Adam: No. Too much happened. The children
5 *were left* / *were leaving* / *left* on their own to do what they wanted. They weren't happy!

Ross: Oh, no! Why did anyone think that was a good idea?

Adam: Well, so many different reality shows
6 *have made* / *have been made* / *have been making* already that they are desperately trying to find something new.

Ross: Hey, that gives me an idea. I have my own
7 *report* / *blog* / *channel*. It **8** *has been read* / *has read* / *has been reading* by eighty-four people so far! My next article will be about new ideas for reality TV shows.

Adam: Great! I'll be the first to read it.

Extra challenge!

6 ★★★ How much do you know? Complete the sentences with the correct form of the verbs from the box. Then circle the correct answers.

- hold • make
- sing • win • ~~write~~

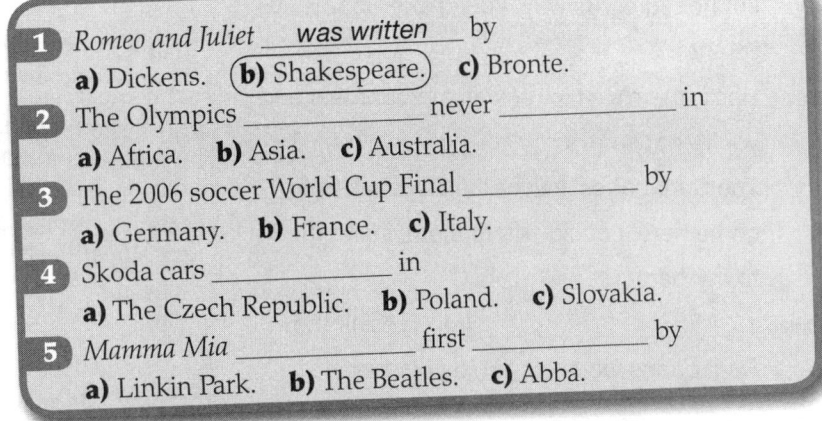

1 *Romeo and Juliet* ___*was written*___ by
   a) Dickens. **b)** Shakespeare. **c)** Bronte.

2 The Olympics _____ never _____ in
   a) Africa. **b)** Asia. **c)** Australia.

3 The 2006 soccer World Cup Final _____ by
   a) Germany. **b)** France. **c)** Italy.

4 Skoda cars _____ in
   a) The Czech Republic. **b)** Poland. **c)** Slovakia.

5 *Mamma Mia* _____ first _____ by
   a) Linkin Park. **b)** The Beatles. **c)** Abba.

Answers 2 a 3 c 4 a 5 c

83

11B He was being chased.

Phrases

1a ★ Circle the correct answers.

a) What (more) / much / many do you want?

b) What's going up / out / on?

c) Dream off / on / out!

d) . . . that way / much / a lot

b ★★ Complete the conversation with the correct phrases from Exercise 1a.

Isabel: Hey, Harry! What are you up to?

Harry: Nothing much. Why?

Isabel: Come to the CD store with me.

Harry: Why? 1 ___What's going on___ ?

Isabel: Robbie Strange is there. He's giving away free copies of his CD.

Harry: Robbie Strange? Here in our town?

Isabel: Yeah, I know. I couldn't believe it. So, do you want to come?

Harry: I'm not sure. Anyway, I don't like Robbie Strange 2 _____ .

Isabel: Harry, there's a big rock star in our town and you're not sure. 3 _____ ?

Harry: The Sugababes! I want the Sugababes to come here! I could talk to them, invite them to my party . . .

Isabel: 4 _____ ! I don't think the Sugababes would come to your party!

Grammar: The passive: present continuous, past continuous, and simple future

2 ★ Complete the conversation with the correct passive form of the verbs in parentheses.

Student: Miss Smith, have you decided who will play Romeo in the school play yet?

Teacher: Yes, Romeo 1 ___will be played___ (play) by Martin Finch. Are the costumes ready?

Student: Not yet. They 2 _____ (finish) as we speak.

Teacher: Why are they taking so long? They 3 _____ (make) three weeks ago.

Student: Don't worry. They 4 _____ (finish) tomorrow.

3 ★★ Complete the newspaper articles with phrases from the box.

- are being looked at
- was being filmed
- will be allowed
- was being driven
- was being followed
- ~~is being examined~~

STAR NEWS

Ted Francis, the *Big Brother* winner, [1]*is being examined* in the hospital today after a car accident. He [2] _____ to the TV studios for a talk show when another car crashed into his. The driver of the other car has been arrested for driving while using a cell phone. According to hospital reports, Ted and his driver [3] _____ to leave the hospital later today.

Model Becky Lester was alone when she realized she [4] _____ by a mugger. Luckily, she [5] _____ secretly by paparazzi. The videos [6] _____ by the police who are trying to see the face of the mugger.

Use your English: Give opinions, agree, and disagree

4 ★ **Complete the conversation with words from the box.**

> • agree • don't • idea • it's
> • mean • ~~think~~ • too • way

Tom: Hello Henry. Do you want to join the debate club with me?

Henry: I don't know. What do you debate? Give me an example.

Tom: OK. I **1** _think_ , we should learn more about politics in school.

Henry: I don't **2** _____ with you. The schedule is full. We can't have fewer math or science classes.

Tom: OK, I see what you **3** _____ . Maybe it shouldn't be a school subject, but I still think politics would be an interesting thing to talk about at school. We could have an after-school politics club.

Henry: Sorry, I **4** _____ agree. I think **5** _____ a terrible **6** _____ . I think we should play more sports or just go home and watch TV.

Tom: Me **7** _____ .

Henry: What? But you said . . .

Tom: I was showing you what the debate club is like. You should come. You're good at it.

Henry: No **8** _____! The only thing I want to debate is which video game to play with my brother.

Consolidation

5 Circle the correct answers.

When a new book **1**____ or people are working on a movie, there has to be great secrecy because, with the Internet, any news of what is happening travels fast.

Before J. K. Rowling **2**____ the last Harry Potter book, hundreds of pages "from the book" **3**____ online. No one knew whether they were real or not. Some people thought that her trash **4**____ by people trying to find notes with ideas on them. The official Harry Potter websites refused to include any "spoilers," information that would spoil the enjoyment of the book. In their opinion, the book should have stayed a secret until it reached stores. Many people **5**____ with them, but others wanted to be the first to know the ending!

Film makers also try to keep things secret. They hire security guards to make sure that only people who **6**____ on a movie can get into the studios while a movie **7**____ . However, there are so many people working on a movie that no one knows if someone **8**____ by the tabloids for information.

1 a) is writing   **b) is being written**   c) was written
2 a) had finished   b) had been finished   c) had been finishing
3 a) were being read   b) had been reading   c) were reading
4 a) was searching   b) searched   c) was being searched
5 a) believed   b) agreed   c) thought
6 a) are being worked   b) are worked   c) are working
7 a) is being made   b) is making   c) makes
8 a) pays   b) is paying   c) is being paid

Grammar: The passive: modals, gerund (-*ing* form), and infinitive

1 ★ Circle the correct verbs.

School rules

1 Uniforms must (be worn) / worn / being worn at all times.
2 Homework should *be done / being done / to do* every day.
3 Teachers and students don't want *being shouted / to be shouted / shouting* at. Please talk calmly and politely at all times.
4 All messages from the school to parents must *to be signed / be signed / be signing* by parents and returned to teachers.
5 Students shouldn't go into the staff room without *being asked / be asked / to be asked*.
6 Tests ought *to mark / be marked / to be marked* and returned to students in one week or less.
7 Ball games mustn't *play / be played / be playing* inside the school building.
8 Tests should *give / be giving / be given* once a term.
9 Students who arrive late will *to be sent / being sent / be sent* to the principal.

2 ★★ Complete the Web comments with the correct passive form of the verbs in parentheses.

interestingopinions

www.interestingopinions.com

The website where you can write your opinions on any topic you like. Click on any statement that you'd like to agree or disagree with and tell us what you think and why.

Education

Some of our teachers look terrible. I think teachers should ¹___be given___ (give) uniforms to wear.

Melanie age 14

We should ²_____ (tell) about tests in advance. Students don't like ³_____ (give) surprise tests.

Dave, age 13

Why aren't there more parents' meetings? Parents want ⁴_____ (tell) about problems quickly.

Cathy, age 14

The media

We need to stop using so much paper and fuel! News should only ⁵_____ (read) online, ⁶_____ (watch) on TV, or ⁷_____ (listen) on the radio.

Keith, age 16

Why do people read tabloid newspapers? They must enjoy ⁸_____ (lie) to!   *Tim, age 15*

Can you believe everything you read on a blog? The information online ought ⁹_____ (check) to make sure it's true.   *Mi Jun, age 15*

Work

It's hard to be a working parent. Parents should ¹⁰_____ (allow) to work from home.

Cherie, age 17

Who says that a movie star is worth more than a nurse? Or a doctor is worth more than a teacher? Everyone should ¹¹_____ (pay) the same wages.

Jack, age 14

I hate wearing a uniform to school and I'm going to hate ¹²_____ (make) to wear a tie at work. People should wear what they like to work.

Chris, age 15

Vocabulary: Adjective and noun formation

3a ★ Write N (noun) or A (adjective).

1 beautiful   _A_
2 greed   ____
3 difference   ____
4 courageous   ____
5 angry   ____

6 wisdom   ____
7 cruelty   ____
8 brave   ____
9 poverty   ____
10 young   ____

b ★ Complete the nouns and adjectives that match the words in Exercise 3a.

1 b_e a u t y_
2 g _ _ _ _ _
3 d _ _ _ _ _ _ _ _
4 c _ _ _ _ _ _
5 a _ _ _ _

6 w _ _ _
7 c _ _ _ _
8 b _ _ _ _ _ _
9 p _ _ _ _
10 y _ _ _ _

4 ★★ Complete the text with the correct form of the words in parentheses.

This year's final of *Our School Has Talent* was very ¹*successful* (success). Ten ² _____ (luck) students tried to show us what they could do. It was a ³ _____ (stress) time for the students who were all ⁴ _____ (hope) that they would win first prize.

Of course, there could only be one winner and that was Kathy Morales, age fourteen. Her obvious ⁵ _____ (confident) helped her, but the fact that she is also an amazing singer and the most talented of the ten meant she was the judges' choice.

Eleven-year-old Luke Wright showed great ⁶ _____ (courageous) competing with students much older than himself. I'm sure he'll be back next year!

Consolidation

5 Complete the text with the correct form of the words from the box.

> • anger • ~~be~~ • be • be • different • greed
> • proud • success • true • wisdom

www.interestingopinions.com/your_views

interestingopinions.com/your_views

The idea about teachers wearing a uniform is great! Our math teacher wears jeans but we can't! I don't like ¹ ____*being*____ told to wear a uniform. The school says we should have ² _____ in our school and the uniform. Well, so should the teachers. It's their school, too. *Natalie, age 14*

www.interestingopinions.com/your_views

I don't agree with the statement that tabloids tell lies. I know they gossip but surely they tell the ³ _____ ? Imagine you were a celebrity and you read lies about yourself in the paper. You'd be really ⁴ _____ and you would do something about it. Just because you're famous and ⁵ _____ doesn't mean people can lie about you. *Keith, age 13*

www.interestingopinions.com/your_views

Mi Jun, I know what you mean about blogs. Just because something is posted online doesn't mean it's true. It isn't ⁶ _____ to believe everything you read. Lies can ⁷ _____ written anywhere. *Dan, age 16*

www.interestingopinions.com/your_views

What a crazy idea that everyone should earn the same money! There's a big ⁸ _____ between the training that a doctor does and a nurse. Of course the doctor gets more. It's not just that people are ⁹ _____ and want tons of money. A doctor has to study for six years or more. They have to borrow money to study and that money has ¹⁰ _____ paid back to the bank. *Susie, age 14*

Nanotechnology

Read

Nanotechnology in fiction

1 ★ Write N (noun) or A (adjective) and then find related words in the dictionary.

1 defense	N	*defendant n – person, defensive a*
2 disaster	☐	_____
3 famous	☐	_____
4 optimistic	☐	_____
5 realistic	☐	_____
6 scientist	☐	_____

2 ★★ Read the text. Complete the blanks (A–F) with the words (1–6) from Exercise 1.

Nanotechnology has many uses and the tiny sizes involved have helped in computer technology, medicine, transportation, and many other areas of modern life. However, not everyone is **A** ___optimistic___ about the future of nanotechnology. Some people worry that it may cause a **B** _____ if it isn't carefully controlled.

Nanotechnology has been a perfect subject for writers and film makers over the last decade. Here are some examples of some of the good and the bad, the serious and the not so serious books, and movies that have been written about it.

Agent Cody Banks was an entertaining but not very **C** _____ movie starring Frankie Muniz as Cody and Hilary Duff as Natalie. Frankie is probably most **D** _____ for the TV show *Malcolm in the Middle*. Hilary Duff is a talented actress and singer.

In the movie, Cody is a fifteen-year-old CIA agent who goes to school with Natalie. Her father works for Dr. Brinkman, who plans to use his nanobots to destroy the world's **E** _____ systems.

Unfortunately, Cody falls in love with Natalie and he tells her everything. Dr. Brinkman finds out and his men knock Cody out, leave him unconscious, and kidnap Natalie. Cody wakes up and finds he is in trouble with the CIA and with his parents because it is very late when he finally gets home. They have no idea that he works for the CIA.

Of course, Cody is the hero in the end and the evil **F** _____, Dr. Brinkman, is stopped, Natalie and her father are saved and Natalie finally falls in love with Cody. A good movie to watch on DVD with the whole family.

More recently, Michael Crichton's novel *Prey*

New words and phrases

3 ★★ Circle the correct meanings.

1 decade
  a) a period of five years   b) a period of two years
  c) a period of ten years *(circled)*

2 knock out (v)
  a) to make a sound with your hand on a surface
  b) win a competition
  c) make someone become unconscious

3 unconscious
  a) awake   b) asleep
  c) in a state like sleep caused by injury

4 kidnap
  a) take someone by force and demand money for
     their return
  b) take someone away from school
  c) take someone by force and then abandon them

Comprehension

4 ★★ Write *T* (true), *F* (false), or *DK* (don't know).

1 The writer doesn't like the movie *Agent Cody Banks*. [F]

2 Frankie Muniz played Cody Banks before he starred in *Malcolm in the Middle*. [ ]

3 Hilary Duff is not only an actress. [ ]

4 Frankie Muniz was fifteen when he made *Agent Cody Banks*. [ ]

5 Dr. Brinkman is Natalie's father. [ ]

6 Natalie falls in love with Cody when she first meets him. [ ]

7 The CIA is unhappy with Cody. [ ]

8 Cody's parents are angry because they don't like him being an agent. [ ]

9 The movie has a happy ending. [ ]

Listen

5 ★ 🎧12 Listen to three people discussing a TV show about nanogenes. Who read about the show but didn't see it?

a) Josie   b) Nick   c) Daryl

6 ★★ 🎧12 Listen again and circle the correct answers.

The Empty Child wearing a gas mask.

1 Josie thought *The Empty Child* was
  a) funny.   b) believable.   c) scary.

2 Daryl thought it was
  a) a war movie.   b) a science-fiction movie.
  c) only for girls.

3 The show was set in
  a) 1914.   b) 1941.   c) 1949.

4 *The Empty Child* was a(n)
  a) soldier.   b) alien.   c) dead boy.

5 The nanogenes came from
  a) a hospital.   b) a bomb.   c) a space ambulance.

6 The nanogenes wanted to
  a) make everyone well.   b) kill everyone on Earth.
  c) go back to their planet.

7 The show can be seen
  a) on TV again.   b) on DVD.   c) on the Internet.

Write

7 ★★ Look at the possible problems associated with nanotechnology. On a separate sheet of paper, write a short article for a newspaper. Look at the title and the information below.

Some people say that nanotechnology can be dangerous. Are they correct?
• Tiny robots can take over the world.
• Governments can use tiny hidden cameras to spy on us.
• We may breathe in small pieces of nanotechnology which could be bad for our health.

There are lots of advantages of using nanotechnology such as ... However, there may be some disadvantages, too. For example ... Another possible danger is that ... Overall, I think that nanotechnology ...

If she hadn't been so generous, . . .

Grammar: Conditional: *if* clause + past perfect

1 ★ Match the beginnings (1–6) with the endings (a–f).

1 If John had been a real friend, he

2 If I had known it was so badly made, I

3 If I had known you wanted one too, I

4 If you hadn't gone to the party, you

5 If we had bought the book on the Internet, it

6 If you had let the paparazzi photograph you, they

a) would have bought two.

b) wouldn't have told everyone your secret.

c) wouldn't have met Cheryl.

d) would have left you alone for the rest of the evening.

e) wouldn't have bought it.

f) would have been much cheaper.

2 ★ Complete the conversations with the correct form of the verbs in parentheses.

Leo's bad day!

1 **Leo:** I lost in the tennis tournament today.

   Tennis coach: I'm not surprised. You didn't train at all. If you ___had trained___ (train), you would have won because you're really good.

2 **Leo:** I can't believe I failed my English test. My essay was really good.

   English teacher: Yes, but you didn't write what I asked you to write. If you _____ (listen), you would have passed.

3 **Leo:** Why aren't I on the school soccer team?

   Soccer coach: If you'd come to the practice game, I _____ (see) how good you are. I can't choose you if I don't see you play.

4 **Leo:** I'm starving. I didn't have any lunch at school today.

   Leo's friend: If you _____ (not buy) chips, you would have had enough money to buy lunch!

5 **Leo:** Why didn't you publish my article in the school newspaper?

   Editor: The newspaper was published today and you gave us your article this morning. If you _____ (give) it to us earlier, we _____ (have) time to put it in the newspaper!

3a ★★ Look at the story.

Tom's lucky day!

Could you get the *Daily News* on your way home, I don't have time.

Sorry, we're sold out of the *Daily News*. The supermarket might have one.

SUPERMARKET

OUR MILLIONTH CUSTOMER WILL WIN $20,000!

Congratulations! You are our millionth customer!

b ★★ Now complete the sentences about the story.

1 Tom's mom / have / more time / not ask/ Tom to get the newspaper

If Tom's mom had had more time, she wouldn't have asked Tom to get the newspaper.

2 Tom's mom / get up / earlier /buy / the newspaper on her way to work

_____

_____

3 the newsstand / have / the *Daily News* / Tom / buy / it there

_____

_____

4 Tom / not go / the supermarket / the man / not tell / him to look there

_____

_____

5 the woman / not drop / her purse / she / enter/ the supermarket before Tom

_____

_____

6 Tom / not win / the money / the woman / go / in before him

_____

_____

Vocabulary: Verbs connected with money

4 ★ Circle the correct answers.

1 How much do you (earn) / afford / inherit in your job?

2 I can't *repay / owe / afford* to buy a new dress.

3 Do you *spend / lend / donate* some of your money to charity?

4 My dad had his own business but it went *bankrupt / owed / debt* last year.

5 Can you *borrow / lend / donate* me five dollars until next week, please?

6 I try to *save / owe / afford* money every month but it's not always possible.

7 You must be crazy to invest *on / in / to* a company that you know nothing about.

8 Malcolm's crazy! He had $500 and he *spent / gave / lent* it all away.

5 ★★ Complete the words.

Help with your money problems

Q: I [1]l *e n t* my friend five dollars last month and he hasn't paid it [2]b _ _ _ yet. What should I do?

A: You should talk to him. He might have forgotten. I'm sure he doesn't want to [3]o _ _ you money.

Q: I [4]w _ _ some money in a competition. My brother wants me to [5]s _ _ _ _ it on video games but I want to [6]s _ _ _ it until the holidays. Now he won't let me use his computer. What should I do?

A: You should keep the money. He'll soon forget and let you use his computer again.

Q: My parents got into [7]d _ _ _ because their business [8]l _ _ _ money. I want to help them. Are there any good ways I can [9]m _ _ _ money without working?

A: No, there aren't! You should get a weekend job. You could [10]e _ _ _ $10 an hour in a café or store.

Consolidation

6 Complete the text with the correct form of the verbs from the box.

> • afford • be • earn • ~~have~~ • have • leave
> • play • spend

In January 2009, the soccer world was shocked by the possible sale of Brazilian star Kaká from Milan to Manchester City. If he [1] *had* moved there, it would [2]_____ been the biggest move in soccer history. Manchester City can now [3]_____ to buy anyone they want because their owner is a billionaire from Dubai. The club [4]_____ $48 million on Robinho but they hadn't finished buying new players. No one knows exactly how much money they offered to Kaká. The tabloids claimed that, if Kaká had [5]_____ Milan and gone to Manchester, he would have [6]_____ $750,000—a week! In the end, Kaká decided not to go. He said he was happy in Milan. He knew that, if he had [7]_____ for Manchester City, he would have [8]_____ at a richer club but a less successful one. He was already a rich man and some things are more important than money.

If only we'd had the money!

Vocabulary: Phrasal verbs with *out*

1 ★ Complete the conversations with the correct form of the verbs from the box.

> • eat • figure • find • leave • point • sell
> • throw • turn

Conversation 1

Anna: What's for dinner, Mom?

Mom: We're going to 1 _____eat_____ out tonight.

Anna: There's some chicken in the refrigerator.

Mom: No, there isn't. It was very old so I
2 _____ it out.

Conversation 2

Teacher: Sean, your homework isn't very good. You
3 _____ out half the exercises
and the ones you did were copied.

Sean: I couldn't do them, sir.

Teacher: I know you find math very difficult but
you should try to 4 _____ out the
answers for yourself.

Sean: Yes, sir.

Conversation 3

Natalie: I went to the theater to try to get some tickets
for the concert before they 5 _____
out but, when I got there, it 6 _____
out that the concert had been canceled.

Trish: What a drag!

Conversation 4

Principal: I'd just like to 7 _____ out to
all the new students that you are not
allowed to leave the school playground
at break times.

Student 1: I wonder why he's telling us this now
after three weeks.

Student 2: Maybe he 8 _____ out that
Chris and Tom go out every day.

2 ★★ Replace the underlined words with a phrasal verb from Exercise 1. Make any other changes that are necessary.

1 Do you want these old magazines? If you don't,
   throw them out
   I'll ~~put them in the trash~~.

2 Can you look in the paper and <u>see</u> what time the movie starts?

3 We're going to <u>go to a restaurant</u> tonight.

4 At the end of the movie, it <u>became clear</u> that the boy was the girl's long lost brother.

5 What's the answer to number three? I can't <u>calculate</u> the answer.

6 You <u>forgot to include</u> half the information in your article.

7 I thought my friends had forgotten me but my mom <u>let me know</u> that my cell phone was turned off.

8 Sorry, the chips are <u>gone</u>. People bought them all.

Grammar: *wish/if only* + past perfect

3a ★ Complete the sentences with the past perfect form of the verbs in parentheses.

1 If only we _had played_ (play) better.

2 I wish I _____ (not add) so much salt.

3 I wish I _____ (not spend) so much on CDs.

4 I wish I _____ (not eat) all that cake.

5 If only I _____ (go) to bed earlier.

6 If only I _____ (not leave) it on the table.

7 If only I _____ (listen) to my teacher.

8 I wish we _____ (bring) a map with us.

b ★★ **Now match sentences (1–8) with problems (a–h).**

a) I'm so tired today. ☐

b) We lost the game. ☐ 1

c) This soup tastes awful now! ☐

d) Someone has stolen my phone. ☐

e) We took the wrong road and now we're lost. ☐

f) I don't have any money left for a burger. ☐

g) It was really creamy and now I feel ill. ☐

h) Now I don't know what exercises to do. ☐

4 ★★ **Read about the famous mistakes. Complete the sentences (1–4) and match them with the correct mistakes (A–D).**

FAMOUS MISTAKES

A In 1984, The Portland Trailblazers had to choose a new basketball player. They chose Sam Bowie and rejected ... Michael Jordan, the most famous player in basketball history.

B The first Harry Potter book was rejected by twelve publishers before Bloomsbury Publishing decided to accept it.

C In 1998, Will Smith was offered the part of Neo in *The Matrix*. He rejected it and decided to make *Wild Wild West* instead. *The Matrix* was a huge success but *Wild Wild West* wasn't very popular.

D In 1997, George Clooney played Batman in the film *Batman and Robin*. In 2008, he was voted the worst ever Batman.

1 only / we know / how popular the books would be

If only we had known how popular the books would be. ☐ B

2 only / I take / the part

_____ ☐

3 only / I not play / that part

_____ ☐

4 wish / we not choose / him

_____ ☐

Consolidation

5 **Complete the conversations with words from the box. Write the verbs in the correct form.**

> • figure out • find out • if • leave
> • ~~not eat out~~ • only • point out • sell out
> • throw out • wish • wish • ~~wish~~

1 **Man:** I *wish* we *hadn't eaten out* tonight.

  Woman: Me, too. This chicken is disgusting.

2 **Joe:** The new sofa is too big for our living room.

  Bob: I know. I noticed it in the store.

  Joe: Well, I _____ you _____ it _____ earlier!

3 **Boy:** Oh, no! We missed the movie.

  Girl: I _____ you _____ the time before we left home!

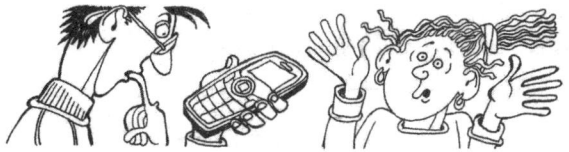

4 **Man:** I can't _____ _____ how to use this phone. If _____ I _____ the instructions.

5 **Salesperson:** I'm sorry. The *Madagascar 2* DVDs just _____.

  Girl: _____ only we _____ _____ home earlier.

Phrases

1 ★ Complete the conversation with phrases from the box.

> • How about it • it's on me • Lead the way
> • Tell me about it • What a pain
> • ~~What are you up to~~

Tom: Hey, Sarah! **1** _What are you up to_ this afternoon?

Sarah: Nothing much. I don't have any money. Going out is so expensive.

Tom: **2** _____! I spent $20 last Friday on nothing.

Sarah: Oh, no! Well, what should we do?

Tom: We could go to Mario's.

3 _____? Don't worry about money, **4** _____.

Sarah: Great. **5** _____! Hey, Mom, I'm going out with Tom.

Mom: Sorry, dear. I have to go out. You'll have to look after your little brother.

Sarah: Oh, no! **6** _____!

Tom: Oh, well. Another time. See you later.

Grammar: Conditional: _if_ clause + _might have_

2 ★ Complete the conversations with the correct form of the verbs in parentheses.

1 Nathan: If you _had arrived_ (arrive) earlier, we _might have gotten_ (might get) tickets for the concert.

Charles: They _____ (might sell) out even if I _____ (arrive) at 8 A.M. but I bought two tickets on the Internet last night!

2 Jenny: It's a shame you couldn't come to the party on Saturday. If you _____ (come), you _____ (might meet) someone nice.

Tanya: Yes, but if I _____ (not meet) anyone nice, I _____ (might spend) all night by myself!

3 Simon: So, what did you think of the movie, Leo?

Leo: Well, it was kind of hard to follow in places.

Simon: I know what you mean. If you _____ (read) the book, you _____ (might understand) the movie.

4 Debbie: If you _____ (check) the time of the movie on the Internet, we _____ (might not miss) the beginning.

Rob: Yes, but if I _____ (turn on) my computer, I _____ (might not leave) the house at all!

3 ★★ Look at the information about the celebrities. Complete the sentences about what they might have done.

Mick Jagger
He studied at the London School of Economics
not join/The Rolling Stones/become/businessman

1 If Mick Jagger _hadn't joined The Rolling Stones, he might have_ become a businessman.

Roger Federer
When he was young he was really good at soccer.
not play/tennis/play professional soccer

2 If Roger Federer _____ _____ professional soccer.

94

Victoria Beckham

She wanted to become a star when she saw the movie *Fame*.

not see/*Fame*/not want/to be a star

3 If Victoria Beckham _____

_____ to be a star.

Brad Pitt

He studied journalism at the University of Missouri.

become a journalist/not start/ acting

4 Brad Pitt _____

_____ acting.

Use your English: Give and accept congratulations

4 ★ Complete the words.

Conversation 1

Lisa: **1** Guess w_hat_! I've been chosen to play the lead part in the school play.

Jackie: Great **2** j_____! That's **3** f_____.

Lisa: Thanks. I couldn't have done it **4** w_____ you. You gave me the confidence to try acting.

Jackie: Don't be **5** s_____. You're so talented. I know you'll be a star!

Conversation 2

Keith: **6** B_____ it or not, my parents have bought me a new computer.

Sam: Wow! **7** T_____ great!

Keith: It must have been my **8** l_____ day.

Consolidation

5 Complete the conversation.

Phil: Hey, guess **1** _what_? I finally found a summer job.

Andy: Congratulations! You **2** _____ be thrilled.

Phil: I am. **3** _____ I hadn't gotten a job, I might **4** _____ have had enough money for a vacation.

Andy: Where are you working?

Phil At a café. Cathy told me about it when I met her at the movies on Friday. If I hadn't **5** _____ to the movies, I might not **6** _____ heard about the job.

Andy: Let's go and celebrate. We could get a burger. How **7** _____ it?

Phil: OK, but you're not paying. It's **8** _____ me. Now that I have a job, I can afford it.

Extra challenge!

6 ★★★ Read the information about Eva Green. Complete the sentences with *might (not) have* or an *if* clause.

- brought up in France
- saw a movie that changed her life at the age of fourteen; decided to become an actress
- was seen by the director of *Casino Royale* in a different movie
- was offered the part of Vesper Lynd in *Casino Royale*
- read the script for *Casino Royale*; thought that Vesper was an interesting character
- agreed to be in *Casino Royale*
- won two awards for *Casino Royale*; became an international star

1 If she hadn't seen a movie that changed her life when she was fourteen, _____

_____.

2 _____,

he might not have asked her to be in *Casino Royale*.

3 _____,

she might not have agreed to be in the movie.

4 If Eva hadn't been in *Casino Royale*, _____

_____.

INTEGRATED CONSOLIDATION SKILLS

The inheritance

Read

1 ★ Read the story quickly. Who died? _____

2 ★★ Read the story again and put the paragraphs (A–D) in the correct order.

A [C] Four years later, a ghost appeared in front of Chaffin's other sons. The ghost looked like James Chaffin and was wearing an old coat that James had worn when he was alive. The ghost told his sons to find the old coat and look inside it carefully. The coat was at Marshall's home so they had to make sure that he wouldn't find out.

B [ ] No one knows the real truth of the story. Some people think that one of the other sons forged the second will and made up the story about the ghosts, but experts said that it was definitely written in James's handwriting. Another theory was that one of the sons might have known about the second will but had forgotten where it was. When he remembered, he made up the ghost story. Perhaps he was embarrassed that he, his mother, and brothers had been living without money for four years. The third theory . . . James's ghost really did come back to tell them about the will.

C [ ] In 1921, in North Carolina, a man named James Chaffin died. He had a wife and four sons. He had written a will in 1905 and it said that all his money should go to his third son, Marshall. No one knew why. His other sons and his wife got nothing and Marshall didn't want to share his inheritance with them. While Marshall and his family were rich, Chaffin's wife and other sons were now very poor.

D [ ] The other sons went to Marshall's house to look for the coat. When they found it, there was a note inside. The note told them to look inside a book which was in their mother's house. There they discovered a newer will which shared the inheritance equally among the three sons and their mother. Marshall was unhappy but he accepted that the will was real.

New words and phrases

3 ★★ Find words in the text to match the definitions.

1 to divide and give out in parts ____share____

2 a written statement that a person leaves after they die _____

3 the spirit of a dead person who appears again

_____

4 in parts which are the same size _____

5 an acceptable explanation that may not be true

_____

Comprehension

4 ★★ Read the story again and answer the questions.

1 When did James write his first will?

_In 1905._____

2 Who got all of James's money in the first will?

_____

3 What did the ghost tell the sons to do and why was this difficult?

_____

4 How was the second will different from the first?

_____

Listen

> **Listening tip: Use the task to guide you**
>
> **Remember!** Before you start to listen, look at the task carefully. Check what information you need to listen for. This will help you to listen more effectively.

5 ★ Look at headings (A–E) below and decide which two ideas the speakers could be talking about.

A Millions of dollars for nothing.

1 A man spent his inheritance but didn't buy anything he could keep.   ✓

2 ~~A family receives a small inheritance.~~   ✗

3 A man paid lawyers a lot of money to fight for an inheritance, but he lost.   ✓

B The inheritance was changed in the end.

1 Someone complained that they should get more of an inheritance, and they won.   ☐

2 One will was found and then, later, a second will was found.   ☐

3 A woman left all her money to her friend who disappeared with the money.   ☐

C Now I want to read it.

1 A person was told about a will, but didn't believe it and asked to see it.   ☐

2 A person saw a show about an inheritance and enjoyed it so wants to read the book.   ☐

3 A person received an inheritance from a relative that they had never heard of before.   ☐

D It didn't last long.

1 A family argued about an inheritance and never spoke to each other again.   ☐

2 A man received his inheritance and soon spent it all.   ☐

3 A TV show about an inheritance wasn't popular and only one episode was shown.   ☐

E A will that was read out in front of a cage.

1 The person inheriting the money was in prison.   ☐

2 The person inheriting the money was old.   ☐

3 The money was left to animals in a zoo.   ☐

6 ★★ 🎧13 You are going to listen to five people talking about inheritances. Match the speakers (1–5) to the correct headings (A–E) in Exercise 5.

Speaker 1 ____   Speaker 2 ____   Speaker 3 ____

Speaker 4 ____   Speaker 5 ____

Write

7 ★ Replace the underlined words with the words and phrases (a–e). Make any other changes necessary.

> a) ~~However~~   b) As far as I'm concerned
>
> c) However   d) In conclusion   e) What's more

1 <u>Although</u> some people say that you should help your children after you die, others say that children should learn to be independent.
Some people say that you should help your children after you die. However, others say that children should learn to be independent.

2 <u>On the other hand</u>, even if you leave your children an inheritance, it doesn't mean that your children won't work hard for themselves.

_____

_____

3 <u>In addition</u>, for most people, an inheritance is quite small and won't change their lives much.

_____

_____

4 <u>To sum up</u>, there are strong arguments for and against leaving inheritances to your children.

_____

_____

5 <u>In my opinion</u>, whatever parents decide to do, they should explain their decision to their children while they are still alive.

_____

_____

8 ★★ On a separate sheet of paper, write an essay arguing that parents *should* or *should not* leave an inheritance to their children. Look at the Writing bank on page 149 of the Student Book and the ideas in Exercise 7 for help.

Grammar Bank

Welcome to the **Grammar Bank!**

- The **Grammar Bank** gives you extra practice for all the grammar points in each unit of the Student Book.

- At the start of each unit in the Grammar Bank, there is a *Grammar Summary* page with examples of all the grammar points from the unit and notes about grammar rules. You can use these to help you when you are doing an exercise and as a check when you are reviewing.

- A set of *Grammar Practice* exercises follows each Grammar Summary. You can use these exercises as a follow-up to the exercises in the Workbook, or you can use them later to help you review.

- At the end of each unit is a *Consolidation* exercise, which covers all the grammar points from the unit.

Grammar Summary

Simple present and present continuous

Simple present
Affirmative
I/You/We/They **go** to school every day.
He/She/It **lives** in Madrid.

Negative
I/You/We/They **don't go** to school in August.
He/She/It **doesn't live** in Madrid.

Questions and short answers
Does he **live** in Madrid? Yes, he **does**. No, he **doesn't**.
Do you **go** to school on Saturdays? Yes, we **do**. No we, **don't**.

Present continuous
Affirmative
I**'m watching** a movie right now.
He/She**'s learning** Spanish this year.
You/We/They**'re watching** TV.

Negative
I**'m not watching** a movie right now.
He/She **isn't learning** Spanish this year.
You/We/They **aren't watching** TV.

Questions and short answers
Are you **going** to the party next week? Yes, **I am**. No, I**'m not**.
Is she **studying** English this year? Yes, she **is**. No, she **isn't**.
Are they **playing** video games? Yes, they **are**. No, they **aren't**.

Tag questions

I'm late, **aren't I**?
You live in Park Road, **don't you**?
Mick doesn't eat meat, **does he**?
Your parents are teachers, **aren't they**?
Lisa isn't coming with us, **is she**?
Tom has my CD, **doesn't he**?
You don't have any money, **do you**?

Notes
Simple present and present continuous
Usage
- We use the simple present for
  - permanent situations.
  - routines.
  - scheduled events in the future.
  - stative verbs.
    Senses: *see, feel, hear, smell, taste*
    Thoughts/ideas: *believe, forget, know, mean, need, prefer, remember, think, understand, want*
    Emotions: *hate, love, like*
- We use the present continuous to talk about
  - events happening now or around now.
  - future arrangements.

Common mistakes
~~*I'm not understanding this exercise.*~~ ✗
I don't understand this exercise. ✓
~~*I spoke to John and we'll meet tomorrow.*~~ ✗
I spoke to John and we're meeting tomorrow. ✓

Tag questions
Usage
- We use tag questions to check or confirm information.
  What's your name? (I don't know your name.)
  *Your name's Chris, **isn't it**?* (I think I know your name but I want to make sure.)
- We use intonation to show how sure we are when we use tag questions.
  Your name's Chris, isn't it? (I'm not sure.)
  Your name's Chris, isn't it? (I know that it is but I want you to confirm it.)

Form
- We put tag questions at the end of a sentence. To form tag questions we use the correct auxiliary verb + the subject pronoun. When the sentence is positive, we use a negative auxiliary. When the sentence is negative, we use a positive auxiliary.

Present perfect and simple past

Present perfect
Affirmative
I**'ve taken** six tests so far.
Our teacher **has given** us lots of homework to do.

Negative
I **haven't seen** this movie.
My mom **hasn't read** any Harry Potter books.

Questions and short answers
Have you **done** your homework? Yes, I **have**. No, I **haven't**.
Has your sister **gone** shopping? Yes, she **has**. No, she **hasn't**.

Simple past
Affirmative
I/You/He/She/It/We/They **took** six tests last month.

Negative
I/You/He/She/It/We/They **didn't watch** TV last night.

Questions and short answers
Did you **do** your homework last night? Yes, I **did**. No, I **didn't**.

Present perfect with *for* or *since*

I**'ve been** at this school **for** three years.
I**'ve been** at this school **since** 2006.
Steve **hasn't e-mailed for** four weeks.
Steve **hasn't e-mailed since** May.

Intensifiers *much*, *a lot*, *a little* with comparative adjectives and adverbs; *(not) as . . . as*

Teaching is **much/far/a lot/a little more rewarding than** office work.
Teaching is**n't as well-paid as** office work.
We work **much/far/a lot/a little more quietly** with our new teacher **than** we did with our old teacher.
Our old teacher didn't explain things **as clearly as** our new teacher does.

Notes
Present perfect and simple past
Usage
- We use the present perfect to connect past events with the present.
  - a past experience
    I**'ve lived** in Madrid.
  - recent actions with a present result
    I**'ve washed** my dad's car.
    (I washed the car in the past. The car was dirty, now it's clean.)
  - things which started in the past and are still true now
    I **have known** Mick for ten years/ages/a long time.
    I**'ve known** Mick since 1999/we were at elementary school.
- We use the simple past to talk about events that are finished.
    I **worked** in a library for three years.
    (I don't work there now.)

Form
- To form the present perfect we use the correct simple present form of *have* + past participle.

Present perfect with *for* or *since*
Usage
- We use the present perfect with *for* or *since* to show how long an action or event has been in progress.
- We use *for* with a period of time and *since* with a point in time.

Intensifiers *much*, *a lot*, *a little* with comparative adjectives and adverbs; *(not) as . . . as*
Usage
- We use intensifiers with comparative adjectives and adverbs to show how similar or different two things are.
  *My new job is **much/far/a lot harder** than my old one.* (a big difference)
  *My new job is **a little harder** than my old one.* (a small difference)
  *My new job is **as hard as** my old one.* (no difference)
- We can use *(not) as . . . as* to avoid using negative adjectives.

Grammar Practice

Simple present and present continuous

1 ★★ Complete the Internet chat using the cues.

> ▼ | _ ■ X
>
> **Jessica:** Hi Nick. What / you do / right now?
> 1 *What are you doing right now?*
> **Nick:** I / listen / my new CD and / I / chat with you!
> 2 _____
> **Jessica:** My dad / cook / dinner today. He / want / me to help him!
> 3 _____
> **Nick:** he / like / cooking?
> 4 _____
> **Jessica:** No. He / not / usually / cook. He / not know / how to turn the oven on!
> 5 _____
> **Nick:** ☺

Tag questions

2 ★★ Complete the questions with tag questions.

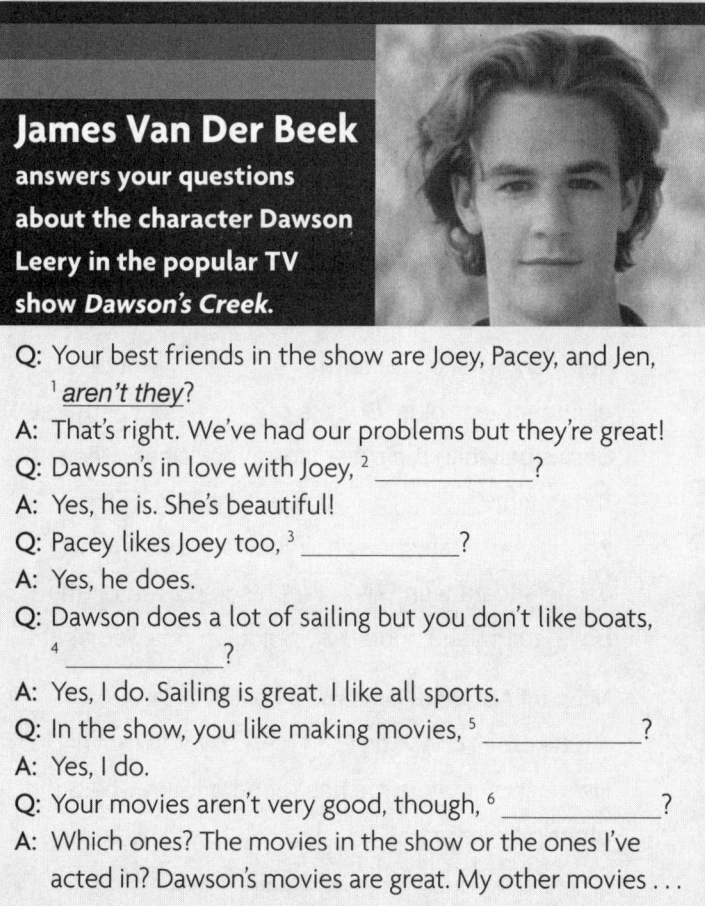

James Van Der Beek
answers your questions
about the character Dawson
Leery in the popular TV
show *Dawson's Creek.*

Q: Your best friends in the show are Joey, Pacey, and Jen,
   ¹ *aren't they*?
A: That's right. We've had our problems but they're great!
Q: Dawson's in love with Joey, ² _____?
A: Yes, he is. She's beautiful!
Q: Pacey likes Joey too, ³ _____?
A: Yes, he does.
Q: Dawson does a lot of sailing but you don't like boats,
   ⁴ _____?
A: Yes, I do. Sailing is great. I like all sports.
Q: In the show, you like making movies, ⁵ _____?
A: Yes, I do.
Q: Your movies aren't very good, though, ⁶ _____?
A: Which ones? The movies in the show or the ones I've
   acted in? Dawson's movies are great. My other movies . . .

Present perfect and simple past

3 ★★ Complete the information about Jack with the present perfect or simple past form of the verbs in parentheses.

1 What *has* Jack's family *done* since last Christmas? (do)
2 Jack's dad *found* a new job in May. (find)
3 He *has worked* in Seattle since July. (work)
4 _____ Jack's family _____ when his dad got a new job? (move)
5 Yes, they _____. They _____ in July. (move)
6 They _____ in Seattle for eight months. (live)
7 Jack _____ a new school in September. (start)
8 He _____ some good friends since September. (make)
9 What other things _____ Jack _____ this year? (do)
10 He _____ the football team. (join)
11 He _____ a part-time job. (start)

Present perfect with *for* or *since*

4 ★★ Complete the sentences 1b–5b and 1c–5c using *for* or *since* so that they mean the same as sentences 1a–5a. Use the correct form of the verbs in parentheses.

1 a) I arrived here at six o'clock. (be)

1 b) I*'ve been here for an* _____ hour.

1 c) I*'ve been here since* _____ seven o'clock.

2 a) I bought this phone three days ago. (have)

2 b) I _____ days.

2 c) I _____ Tuesday.

3 a) Steve met Rebecca on November 10. (know)

3 b) Steve _____ November 10.

3 c) Steve _____ five days.

4 a) I started this job six months ago. (work)

4 b) I _____ months.

4 c) I _____ October.

5 a) I woke up two hours ago. (be awake)

5 b) I _____ hours.

5 c) I _____ 8:00.

Intensifiers *much, a lot, a little* with comparative adjectives and adverbs; *(not) as . . . as*

5 ★ Complete the sentences using the cues.

1 more / staying / interesting / a weekend job / than / is / at home / far

Doing *a weekend job is far more interesting than staying at home* _____ .

2 job / well-paid / as / as / my dad's / isn't

My mom's _____ .

3 little / exciting / the Internet / are / more / a / than

Video games _____ .

4 a / stressful / teaching class 6B / than / our class / lot / more / is

Teaching _____ .

5 as / in the stores / as / the market / expensive / are / the clothes

The clothes in _____ .

Consolidation

6 Complete the text with the correct form of the verbs and adjectives in the box.

> • appear • as • be • fast • for • good • high
> • lot • ~~since~~ • tall

Jaime Nared

Jaime Nared is thirteen years old and she's already over six feet tall! Jaime has played basketball **1** *since* she was four years old and she now plays basketball for Team Concept. The team plays in a special league for future basketball stars. Jaime **2** _____ several times on ABC and CNN TV.

Jaime is amazing! She's much **3** _____ than her friends. She's as tall **4** _____ a lot of eighteen-year-olds. She's a **5** _____ better at basketball than the other kids in her class. She can run much **6** _____ and no one can jump as **7** _____ as she can. In her last girls' game, Jaime's team won 90–7. When she played on the boys' team, she scored 30 points in one game!

Michael Abraham is Jaime's coach. He **8** _____ a basketball coach **9** _____ over thirty years. He's happy that Jaime has found a team where the other players are as **10** _____ as she is.

Grammar Summary

Simple past

Regular verbs
Affirmative
I/You/He/She/It/We/They **moved** last year.
Negative
I/You/He/She/It/We/They **didn't move** last year.
Questions and short answers
Did you **move** last year? Yes, I **did**. No, I **didn't**.

Irregular verbs
Affirmative
I/You/He/She/It/We/They **won** the race yesterday.
Negative
I/You/He/She/It/We/They **didn't win** the race yesterday.
Questions and short answers
Did he **bring** his CDs? Yes, he **did**. No, he **didn't**.
Wh- questions
What movie **did** you **see** last night?

Past continuous and simple past with *while* and *when*

Past continuous + simple past with *while* and *when*
While I **was walking** home, I **saw** an accident.
I **saw** an accident **while** I **was walking** home.

When I **left** home, my dad **was eating** breakfast.
My dad **was eating** breakfast **when** I **left** home.

Simple past + simple past with *when*
When Tom **stood up**, his bag **fell** to the floor.
Tom's bag **fell** to the floor **when** he **stood up**.

Simple past and past perfect

By the time Jack **arrived**, his friends **had left**.
By the time Maria **started** college, she **had saved** over $750.
I **hadn't heard** any *Jet* songs until my friend **gave** me his CD.
A: Nick **came** home really late last night.
B: Where **had** he **been**?

after/before + gerund (-*ing* form)

After finishing his homework, Ben wrote his blog.
Before buying a new computer, I looked at prices on the Internet.

Notes
Simple past
Usage
- We use the simple past to talk about single, completed actions in a completed time period in the past.
- We can sometimes use the simple past without a past time expression when the speaker and listener both know what the time period is.
  Did you see Mission Impossible?
  (they both know it was on TV last night)

Past continuous and simple past with *while* and *when*
Usage
- We use the past continuous and simple past together to talk about an action that happened while another action was in progress. We use the past continuous for the longer action and the simple past for the shorter finished action.
- We use *while* before the past continuous. We use *when* before the simple past.
- Sometimes we can see the same activity as an activity in progress or a single event. We can choose which tense to use.
- We can use simple past + simple past with *when* if two actions occur at the same time in the past.

Simple past and past perfect
Usage
- We use the past perfect with the simple past to show that one past action or event happened before another.
- We often use the past perfect to clarify the order of events.

after/before + gerund (-*ing* form)
Usage
- We can use *after/before* + gerund instead of the simple past or past perfect.

2 Grammar Practice

Simple past

1 ★ Complete the questions and answers with the correct form of the verbs from the box.

• go • leave
• ~~take~~ • win

Around the World in 80 Days

1 How many days ___did___ Phileas Fogg
___take___ to travel around the world?
He ___took___ 80 days to travel around the world.

2 How much money _____ he _____
from his friends?
He _____ £20,000 (about $31,398).

3 What date _____ he _____ England?
He _____ England on October 2, 1872.

4 Where _____ he _____ first?
He _____ to Suez first.

2 ★★ Complete the sentences to correct these statements.

1 He traveled with a man named James Foster.
He ___didn't travel___ with James Foster. He
___traveled___ with Passepartout.

2 The detective, Fix, thought that Fogg was a bank manager.
He _____ Fogg was a bank manager.
He _____ he was a bank robber.

3 Fogg married an American woman.
He _____ an American woman. He
_____ an Indian woman.

4 Fogg arrived in London one day late.
He _____ one day late. He _____
one day early.

3 ★★ Write sentences using the cues.

1 My parents and I / not go / to the beach / for vacation. We / go / to the mountains.
My parents and I didn't go to the beach for
vacation. We went to the mountains.

2 Meg and Holly / not take / the bus to school.
They / take / the train.
_____
_____

3 Paulo / see / the concert on TV last night? / No, /
he / see / it on his computer.
_____
_____

4 Tyler / break nose / in / a basketball game? / No, /
he / break his nose / riding his bike.
_____
_____

Past continuous and simple past with *while* and *when*

4 ★ Complete the sentences with the two verbs in the past continuous or the simple past.

1 While Jake *was lying* (lie) on the beach, his
friends *played* (play) soccer

2 Jade _____ (talk) to her friends when
her mom _____ (ask) her to help make
dinner.

3 When Chris _____ (get) to school, the
other students _____ (watch) a movie.

4 As I _____ (wait) for the bus, I _____
(meet) a really cool girl.

5 Eva nearly _____ (have) an accident as
she _____ (ride) her bike home.

6 My friends _____ (wait) for me while I
_____ (try) on some clothes in the store.

7 When Tom _____ (leave) the party, his
friends _____ (decide) to go home, too.

104

Simple past and past perfect

5 ★ Complete the endings (a–e) with the verbs in the past perfect form. Then match the beginnings (1–5) to the endings (a–e).

1 I felt sick because `c`

2 I lost the tennis match because ☐

3 I was tired on Monday because ☐

4 My mom was pleased with me because ☐

5 I couldn't reach my friend Luke because ☐

---
a) I _____ (not practice) enough.

b) he _____ (not turn on) his phone.

c) I _____*had eaten*_____ (eat) too much.

d) I _____ (go) to bed late on Sunday.

e) I _____ (clean) my room and she _____ (not ask) me to do it!

---

after/before + gerund (*-ing* form)

6 ★ Complete the sentences using the information.

1 Event 1: We bought a lot of presents.

Event 2: We got on the plane.

Before _____*getting on the plane, we bought*_____ a lot of presents.

2 Event 1: We spent all our money.

Event 2: We had to walk home.

After _____ _____ walk home.

3 Event 1: We finished the exercise.

Event 2: We left the classroom.

After _____ _____ the classroom.

4 Event 1: Adam cleaned his room.

Event 2: He cooked dinner.

After _____ _____ dinner.

5 Event 1: I had never been in the hospital.

Event 2: I had a bike accident.

Before _____ _____ in the hospital.

Consolidation

7 Circle the correct answers.

Eric: Hi, Alfie. Welcome to San Diego. How was the trip?

Alfie: Hi, Eric. It was a little tiring. We **1** ____ Seattle twenty-four hours ago.

Eric: Was the bus comfortable?

Alfie: Yes, it was OK. Before **2** ____ home, I **3** ____ an MP3 player so I listened to music.

Eric: Was there anyone sitting next to you?

Alfie: Yes, but only at the end. **4** ____ we left Seattle, the seat was empty but we stopped in San Francisco and more people got on. The woman who sat next to me **5** ____ a huge picnic for the trip. After **6** ____ down, she got out a basket full of bread, cheese, meat, and other things. I **7** ____ for hours and I was really hungry. I **8** ____ there, looking at her food when she **9** ____ me to eat with her. It was delicious.

Eric: I hope you **10** ____ too much. My mom has dinner waiting when we get home!

1 a) had left   b) were leaving   c) leaving   (d) left)

2 a) left   b) leaving   c) had left   d) were leaving

3 a) bought   b) was buying   c) had bought
   d) have bought

4 a) When   b) While   c) During   d) From

5 a) was bringing   b) had brought   c) has brought
   d) brings

6 a) sat   b) had sat   c) was sitting   d) sitting

7 a) hadn't eaten   b) didn't eat   c) haven't eaten
   d) wasn't eating

8 a) had been sitting   b) have sat   c) was sitting
   d) am sitting

9 a) invited   b) had invited   c) was inviting
   d) invites

10 a) hadn't eaten   b) weren't eating   c) don't eat
   d) didn't eat

Future tenses: *will*, *be going to*, present continuous form

will

Affirmative

I/You/He/She/It/We/They**'ll (will) meet** you outside.

Negative

I/You/He/She/It/We/They **won't (will not)** travel by plane.

Questions and short answers

Will they **travel** by car? Yes, they **will**. No, they **won't**.

be going to

Affirmative

I**'m going to visit** my grandparents this week.
He/She**'s going to study** English.
You/We/They**'re going to buy** a new computer this year.

Negative

I**'m not going to visit** my grandparents this week.
He/She **isn't going to study** English.
You/We/They **aren't going to buy** a new computer this year.

Questions and short answers

Is she **going to see** her teacher? Yes, she **is**. No, she **isn't**.
Are we **going to watch** a DVD tonight?
Yes, we **are**. No, we **aren't**.

Present continuous form

Affirmative

I**'m meeting** Mark at 3:00.

Negative

He/She/It **isn't coming** to the movies with us.

Questions and short answers

Are you **staying** in a hotel in the summer?
Yes, we **are**. No, we **aren't**.

be about to + infinitive

Quick! The movie **is about to start**.
Our train **is just about to leave**.

Gerund (*-ing form*) as subject

Watching TV is a waste of time.
Working on the weekend is difficult.

Notes

Future tenses: *will*, *be going to*, present continuous form

Usage

- We use *will* to talk about something we think, believe, or know will happen in the future. We can use *will be* for future facts.
- We can use *will* when we suddenly decide to do something.
- We use *going to* for plans, intentions, and predictions in the future based on present evidence.
- We use the present continuous for fixed plans and arrangements in the future.
- We can often use more than one future form.
  Prediction: ***You'll/You're going to have a great time in Italy.***
  Arrangements: ***I'm meeting/I'm going to meet*** John later.
- When we use *going to* with the verb *to go*, we usually omit *to go*.
  I'm going ~~to go~~ **shopping** later.

Common mistakes

~~I'll play tennis with Tom this afternoon.~~ ✗
I'm playing tennis with Tom this afternoon. ✓
~~I'm going to make you a cup of tea if you want.~~ ✗
I'll make you a cup of tea if you want. ✓

be about to + infinitive

Usage

- We use to *be about to* + infinitive to talk about things that are going to start very soon.

Gerund (*-ing* form) as subject

Usage

- We can use the gerund (*-ing* form) when the word is the subject of the sentence. It can explain things or explain why someone does something.

must, need, should, ought to, have to, had better

Obligation
You **must try** harder next year.
You **mustn't be** rude to your friends.
I **have to be** at school at 8:30 tomorrow.

No obligation
We **don't have to/don't need to pay** for the hotel until we arrive.

Advice
You **should wear** something clean to the interview.
You **ought to do** more exercise.
We**'d better leave** soon.
You**'d better not be** late for school again.

make, let, allowed to

Affirmative
My dad **makes me clean** my shoes every day.
My parents **let me watch** TV for one hour a day.
I**'m allowed to wear** what I want on the weekend.

Negative
My parents **don't make me help** with dinner.
My mom **doesn't let me go** out during the week.
I**'m not allowed to eat** fast food.

Notes

must, need, should, ought to, have to, had better

Usage
- We use *must* and *have to* for obligation and necessity.
- We often use *must* when an obligation comes from the speaker.
- We use *mustn't* for things that we can't do and with negative obligations. *Mustn't* is formal. *Can't* is a less formal way to express negative obligation.
- There is no past form of *must* so we use the past form of *have to* for obligation and no obligation in the past.
- *must* and *have to* have different meanings in negative sentences: *don't have to* = no obligation; *mustn't* = it's against the rules.
- We use *should/shouldn't* and *ought to/ought not to* for giving advice, making suggestions, and saying what is right and wrong.
- We use *don't have to/don't need to* when something is not necessary.
- We use *have to* for obligations that come from other people.
- We use *'d better (not)* to give slightly stronger advice.

Form
- We use *must, need, should, ought to, have to, had better* + infinitive without *to*.
- To form negatives, we add *not (n't)* to *must, should, ought to, had better*; we add *don't* to *have to*. We can add *n't* or *don't* to make *need* negative. When we use *needn't*, we follow it with the infinitive without *to*. After *don't need*, we use infinitive + *to*.

make, let, allowed to

Usage
- We use *make* for things we are told we have to do.
- We use *let* and *allowed to* for things that someone says we can do.

Form
- We can use *make* and *allowed to* in the active and passive forms.

Future tenses: *will, be going to,* present continuous form

1 ★ Circle the correct answers.

1 A: I can't do this homework.

  B: (*I'll help*) / *I'm going to help* you if you want.

2 Mr. Smith always gives difficult tests so I'm sure this one *is going to be* / *is being* difficult, too.

3 Look at those black clouds. It's *raining* / *going to rain* soon.

4 Who do you think *is winning* / *will win* the game this afternoon?

5 You look nice. *Are you going out* / *Will you go out* tonight?

2 ★★ Look at the notes and complete the sentences with the correct form of the verbs.

> My plans: finish homework quickly.
>
> Arrangements: Meet friends at 7 P.M. outside the theater.
>
> Prediction: Mark and Dan - arrive late (as usual).
>
> Prediction: Good movie - all the reviews say so.

When I get home, I **1** *'m going to finish* my homework quickly because **2** I _____ my friends at 7:00 outside the theater. Mark and Dan **3** _____ late (as usual) and we'll have to run in to see the start of the movie. But I'm sure it **4** _____ a good movie because all the reviews are very positive.

be about to + infinitive

3 ★ Look at the information and complete the sentences.

1 It's 2:53 and the game starts at 2:55

  The game _____ *is about to start* _____.

2 It's 2:59 and the class ends at 3:00.

  The class _____

  _____.

3 It's Sunday evening and the TV contest starts on Monday.

  The TV contest _____

  _____.

4 Your friend calls just as you open the front door to go out.

  I _____

  _____ the house.

5 Your friend is trying to take a photo and isn't looking where she's going. She's in danger of falling into a hole in the road.

  Look out! You _____

  _____ a hole in the road!

Gerund (*-ing* form) as subject

4 ★★ Put the verbs in parentheses into the correct form and then match the beginnings (1–5) to the endings (a–e).

1 *Working* (Work) on the weekend | c |

2 _____ (Wear) a uniform | |

3 _____ (Listen) to an MP3 player | |

4 _____ (Travel) by plane | |

5 _____ (Eat) a lot of candy | |

a) is quicker than traveling by car.

b) can be bad for your ears.

c) is a good way to earn money.

d) is bad for your teeth.

e) is normal for police officers.

must, need, should, ought to, have to, had better

5 ★★ **Complete the conversation with words from the box.**

> • better • don't • have • need
> • ~~not~~ • ought • to

Ellie: Hi Mia.

Mia: Oh, hello. What time is it? You woke me up.

Ellie: It's 7:30. You'd better 1 _**not**_ be late today. It's the school trip to Seattle. We have 2 _____ be at school by 8:30.

Mia: Why do we 3 _____ to be there so early?

Ellie: The bus is leaving at 9:00 and it won't wait.

Mia: I don't have any money for the bus.

Ellie: You 4 _____ have to pay for the bus but you 5 _____ to bring something to eat.

Mia: They 6 _____ to stop at a café. I don't want to eat sandwiches.

Ellie: You'd 7 _____ ask your mom for something different. I'm bringing a banana and a yogurt.

Mia: Too healthy! I'll take some chips and chocolate.

make, let, allowed to

6 ★★ **Complete the sentences using make, let, or allowed to so they mean the same as the originals.**

1 I have to go to bed at 10:00. Can you stay up late?

My parents _____make me go_____ to bed at 10:00. Are _you allowed to stay up_ late?

2 How often do you have to clean your room?

How often _____ your parents _____ your room?

3 I can't watch more than one hour of TV a day. How much TV can you watch?

I'm _____ more than one hour of TV a day. How much TV are _____ every day?

4 I can't go out during the week.

My parents don't _____ during the week.

5 My mom gives me money for clothes and I can wear what I want. Can you?

My mom _____ what I want. Are _____ anything you like or _____ your parents _____ you wear clothes that they like?

Consolidation

7 **Circle the correct answers.**

> From: Matt
>
> To: Harry
>
> Dear Harry,
>
> I just got a new part-time job. I wash cars! It's great. I 1 _____ to get up early because I don't start work until 11:00. I only work on Saturdays but I've decided that 2 _____ to start working on Sundays, too.
>
> I think that, by the summer, 3 _____ about $700. I 4 _____ to Greece in July with my family. 5 _____ great! 6 _____ spend my money on diving lessons. I'll be fifteen in June so I can get an Open Water Certificate. Then I can dive on my own. We booked our vacation online. 7 _____ vacations on the Internet is so easy.
>
> Anyway, I hope all is well. 8 _____ go because we are 9 _____ have lunch. You 10 _____ to get a part-time job. It's much better than playing video games all day.
>
> See you soon!
>
> Matt

1 a) must   b) need   c) don't have

2 a) I'll   b) I'd better c) I'm going

3 a) I'll have b) I'm having c) I must have

4 a) 'll go   b) 'm going   c) should go

5 a) It'd better be b) It's being c) It'll be

6 a) I'm going to b) I'll   c) I ought to

7 a) Choosing   b) To choose   c) Choose

8 a) I'll   b) I'd better c) I don't have to

9 a) about to   b) going   c) need to

10 a) should   b) must   c) ought

Present perfect with *already, before, never, ever, yet*

Affirmative
We**'ve seen** this movie **already**.

Negative
Mark **hasn't played** guitar in a concert **before**.
Tom **has never failed** a test.
I **haven't called** Beth **yet**.

Questions and short answers
Have you **ever had** an accident at school?
Yes, I **have**. No, I **haven't**.
Has the concert **started yet**?
Yes, it **has**. No, it **hasn't**.

Superlatives with the present perfect

This is **the best** present **I've ever had**.
What's **the hottest** place you**'ve been** to?

Present perfect and present perfect continuous with *for* and *since*

Present perfect
I've known Maria **for** three years.
Have you **known** her **for** a long time?
Have you **known** her **since** you were children?

Present perfect continuous
Tim**'s been playing** guitar **since** he was seven.
Have you **been waiting** here **for** a long time?
Has he **been playing** guitar **since** he was a young boy?

Notes
Present perfect with *already, before, never, ever, yet*
Usage
- We use the present perfect with
  - *already* in positive sentences to emphasize that something has happened before.
  - *before* in negative sentences to say that this is the first time something has happened.
  - *never* in positive sentences to mean *not ever*. We often add *before* to emphasize the sentence.
  - *ever* when we ask *Have you ever. . .* to mean *at any time in your life*.
  - *yet* at the end of questions and negatives to mean *until now*.

Form
See Unit 1, page 100.

Common mistakes
~~I haven't never seen so much food.~~ ✗
I've never seen so much food. ✓
~~Did you ever win a competition?~~ ✗
Have you ever won a competition? ✓

Superlatives with the present perfect
Usage
- We use superlatives with the present perfect to describe things that have happened to us.

Present perfect and present perfect continuous with *for* and *since*
Usage
- We use the present perfect and present perfect continuous with *for* and *since* to show the duration of an action or event.
- We use *for* with a period of time up to the present: *for three years*.
- We use *since* to show the exact point of time in the past when the action or event started: *since last year, since April*.

Form
- To form the present perfect continuous we use *have/has* + *been* + gerund (*-ing* form) of the verb.

Present perfect for numbers and amounts

Connie **has won lots** of prizes for her school work.
Matt **has written three** books.
How many tests **have** you **taken** so far this week?

Relative clauses

Restrictive relative clauses

people (who/that)
He's the guitarist **who/that** played on Eminem's last album.
places (where)
This is the place **where** we first met.
things (which/that)
Is this the sweater **which/ that** you wanted to buy?
possessions (whose)
This is the girl **whose** friends have made a CD.

Nonrestrictive relative clauses

people (who)
My dad, **who** is a teacher, always checks my homework.
places (where)
The hotel, **where** we stayed last summer, was in the city
　center.
things (which)
This CD, **which** I bought last week, is really good.
possessions (whose)
Jackie Dawes, **whose** mom sometimes appears on TV, wants
　to be an actress.

Notes

Present perfect for numbers and amounts

Usage

- We use the present perfect to answer the question *How much/many* in unfinished time periods, e.g. *in your life, this week.*

  How many countries have you been to? (in your life)

Common mistakes

How many books have you been reading this vacation? ✗
How many books have you read this vacation? ✓

Relative clauses

Usage

- We use restrictive relative clauses with *who/that, where, which/that,* or *whose* to add essential information to a clause so that it is clear what we are talking about.

- We use nonrestrictive relative clauses with *who, where, which,* and *whose* to add extra information to a sentence. This information is not essential to the understanding of the sentence and the sentence still makes sense if you remove the clause.

Form

- In restrictive relative clauses, when *who, which,* or *that* refers to the object, we can leave it out.

- In restrictive relative clauses, it is not possible to leave out *whose* or *where.*

- A nonrestrictive relative clause is separated from the main information by a comma or, if it is in the middle of a sentence, two commas.

Common mistakes

Brad Pitt, that was born in Oklahoma, is one of my favorite actors. ✗
Brad Pitt, who was born in Oklahoma, is one of my favorite actors. ✓
This is the dress, which I wore to the party. ✗
This is the dress which I wore to the party. ✓

Grammar Practice

Present perfect with *already, before, never, ever, yet*

1 ★ Put the word in parentheses into the correct place in the sentence.

already

1 Tommy is only four but he's learned how to write ∧

   his name. (already)

2 Have you decided what to wear to school? (yet)

3 I've bought anything from eBay. (never)

4 Have you ridden a horse? (ever)

5 I haven't traveled by plane. (before)

2 ★★ Complete the conversation with the simple past or present perfect form of the verbs in parentheses. Put the time expressions in the correct place.

Hannah: Hi James. Do you want to meet tomorrow?

James: OK.

Hannah: What do you want to do?

James: 1 ____*Have*____ you ____*ever done*____ (ever/do) any fishing?

Hannah: I 2 _____ (go) fishing once last year with my brother. It was so boring.

James: It isn't boring. I 3 _____ (join) a fishing club last week. It's great.

Hannah: 4 _____ you _____ (ever/catch) anything?

James: Well, not exactly. I 5 _____ a fish _____ (not catch/yet) but I 6 _____ (catch) an old shoe yesterday! I 7 _____ all the equipment _____ (not buy/yet). I'm going shopping later to buy everything I need. I 8 _____ my brother _____ (watch/ before) with his friends, though.

Hannah: I 9 _____ (start) a new hobby, too. My parents 10 _____ (buy) me a really good camera for my birthday last month. I 11 _____ (already/ take) a lot of photos. I want to post my work on the school blog but I 12 _____ any really special ones _____ (not take/yet).

James: So, come and take a photo of me catching a giant fish! That would be a great photo for the school newspaper!

Superlatives with the present perfect

3 ★★ Write sentences using the cues. Use a superlative and the present perfect.

1 I climbed Ben Nevis. It is a very high mountain. (high / mountain / climb)

   Ben Nevis is the highest mountain I've ever _____
   climbed. _____

2 I read *Inkheart*. It's really interesting. (*Inkheart* / interesting / read)

   _____
   _____

3 I just played my new video game. I've never played a more exciting game. (It / exciting / play)

   _____
   _____

4 I heard the album. Track 3 is an awesome song. (Track 3 / best / hear)

   _____
   _____

5 I watched the movie *Salt*. It was so exciting! (*Salt* / exciting / see)

   _____
   _____

Present perfect and present perfect continuous with *for* and *since*

4 ★★ Write questions and answers.

America Ferrera
- Started acting: age 8
- First TV appearance: nine years ago
- *Ugly Betty* started: 2006
- Met hubby Ryan Williams: at college

1 Q: long / she / act / ?

How long has she been acting?

  A: *She's been acting since she was eight.*

2 Q: long / she / be / a TV star / ?

  _____

  A: _____

3 Q: long / she / playing / *Ugly Betty* / ?

  _____

  A: _____

4 Q: long / she / know / Ryan Williams / ?

  _____

  A: _____

Present perfect for numbers and amounts

5 ★★ Write questions and answers.

Birgit:

movies – 15

awards – 2

earnings – $10,000,000

1 Q: How / movies / Birgit / make / ?

  _____

  A: _____

2 Q: How / awards / Birgit / win / ?

  _____

  A: _____

3 Q: How / money / she / earn / ?

  _____

  A: _____

Relative clauses

6 ★ Complete the letter with the clauses (a–f) in the correct place.

a) who you met last year
b) ~~that you sent me for my birthday~~
c) whose record is 11–0
d) which is the best grade I've ever had
e) that Mom and Dad gave me
f) which was fun

Dear Grandma and Grandpa,

Thank you very much for the money [1] *b*. I added it to some money [2] ____ and bought a new game for my computer. I had a good birthday. I had a party here at home, [3] ____. Ten friends came. My best friend Jake, [4] ____, stayed for the night.

School is going well. I got an 85 on a math test, [5] ____. I'm also on the school baseball team now. Next week, we're playing against Stoke Park school, [6] ____!

Thanks again. See you in the summer!

Love, Harry

Consolidation

7 Complete the record review with words from the box.

- already • ~~been~~ • before • ever • since
- which • who • whose • yet

I've [1] *Been* ***Waiting* by Fighting Talk**

This single, [2] _____ is Fighting Talk's fifth, is great. In fact, it's the best single they've [3] _____ made. Lead singer, Meg, [4] _____ voice is sometimes too quiet, is awesome. I've never heard her sing like this [5] _____. Max, [6] _____ has been playing the guitar [7] _____ he was eleven, sounds great. Leo is much better than the old drummer. In fact, I've [8] _____ forgotten the last drummer's name! The stores haven't started selling this record [9] _____ but you can buy the single online. I'm sure it will be number one very soon.

Conditionals with *if, unless, provided that, as long as*

Affirmative

If I/you/we/they **leave** now, I/you/we/they**'ll arrive** on time.

If he/she/it **stops** now, he/she/it**'ll be** late.

I/You/He/She/We/They**'ll have** a picnic on the beach **unless** it **rains**.

I/He/She/We/They**'ll let** you have a party **provided that** you **clean up** after it.

I/He/She/We/They**'ll go** with you **as long as** the tickets **are** free.

Negative

If you **don't work** hard, you **won't get** a good grade on your test.

I won't help you with your homework **unless** you **try** to do it yourself first.

Provided that students **attend** all classes, they **won't have** problems on the test.

You **won't have** any problems with your test **as long as** you **study** hard.

Questions and short answers

Will it **be** a problem **if** we **have** an end-of-year dance?

Yes, it **will**. No, it **won't**.

Future time clauses with *when, until, as soon as, by the time, before*

when and *as soon as*

I'll go out with my friends **when** I **finish** my homework.

As soon as/When we hear the bell, we**'ll leave** the room.

until

We **won't call** you **until** we **arrive**.

by the time

By the time John **arrives**, the movie **will be** over.

before

I'll finish my homework **before** I **watch** TV.

in case + simple present

Take your cell phone with you **in case** you **want** to call us later.

Tom always has two alarm clocks on in the morning **in case** one **doesn't work**.

Notes

Conditionals with *if, unless, provided that, as long as*

Usage

- We use
  - the conditional tenses to talk about something that may happen in the future as a result of something else happening (or not happening).
  - *if/provided that/as long as* for the result of an action happening.
  - *unless* for the result of an action not happening; *unless* has a similar meaning to *if not*.

Form

- There are two parts in a conditional sentence. We use *if/unless/provided that/as soon as* + simple present for the condition. We use *will* + infinitive without *to* for the result.

Future time clauses with *when, until, as soon as, by the time, before*

Usage

- We use *will* with *when, until, as soon as, by the time, before* to show that
  - something will happen at a specific time in the future.
  - two future events will happen at almost the same time or one immediately after the other.
  - one thing will happen very quickly after the other.

Form

- There are two parts in a future time clause. We use *will* + infinitive without *to* for the result. We use *when, until, as soon as, by the time, before* + simple present for what happens first.
- The *will* clause can be positive or negative; the *when, until, as soon as, by the time, before* clause is usually positive.

in case + simple present

Usage

- We use *in case* + simple present to say what we do now because something bad might happen later.

Grammar Practice

Conditionals with *if, unless, provided that, as long as*

1 ★ Complete the sentences with *if, unless, provided that,* or *as long as*.

1 Your computer will work for a few more years ___as long as___ you're careful with it.

2 We'll be ready soon _____ something goes wrong.

3 I'll order pizza for dinner _____ I can find the telephone number of the pizza restaurant.

4 You can go on vacation with your friends _____ you promise to call every day.

5 _____ the weather's nice, we'll go camping.

6 _____ the water's clean, we can go swimming in the lake.

7 _____ someone helps me, I'll cook dinner.

8 _____ you know of a better hostel, I think we should stay here.

2 ★★ Complete the sentences so that they mean the same as the originals using the words in parentheses.

1 If Class 5B works hard for the rest of the semester, I will take them on a trip to Seattle. (provided that)

I will *take Class 5B on a trip to Seattle provided that they work* hard for the rest of the semester.

2 Of course, I won't organize this trip if you don't like the idea. (unless)

Of course, the trip won't happen _____ _____ the idea.

3 The trip can happen if 75% of parents agree. (as long as)

The trip _____ _____ 75% of parents agree.

4 Students will be allowed to go if they bring in a signed letter from their parents. (unless)

Students _____ they bring in a signed letter from their parents.

5 I'll be happy to answer any questions you have about the trip. (if)

_____, _____ happy to answer them.

Future time clauses with *when, until, as soon as, by the time, before*

3 ★ Circle the correct answers.

	From:	Sadie
≡▼	To:	Hannah

Hi Hannah,

Thanks for your e-mail. I'm really excited! I'm going to the Czech Republic with my parents soon. I'd like to learn some Czech [1] (*before*) / *when* / *as soon as* we leave, but I don't have time. I'm definitely going to take my laptop. I know exactly what will happen (because it always does!). Before the plane [2] *is taking* / *will take* / *takes* off, my dad will tell us all what we have to do and see on the first day. [3] *Until* / *By the time* / *As soon as* the plane lands, he'll feel a little tired and as soon as we [4] *get* / *will get* / *are getting* to the hotel, he'll say that he needs "a few minutes to rest." [5] *When* / *Until* / *By the time* my dad falls asleep, [6] *I go* / *I'm going* / *I'll go* on the Internet and try to find some cool places to visit. I know a website that tells you about places that tourists don't usually see. Of course, I [7] *don't* / *'m not* / *won't* really know what these places are like [8] *until* / *when* / *by the time* I see them but it's a really cool site. When Dad [9] *woke* / *wakes* / *will wake* up, I'll know exactly where to go!

I'll tell you all about it [10] *until* / *when* / *by the time* I get back!

Sadie

4 ★★ Rewrite the sentences so that they mean the same as the originals using the time expressions in parentheses.

1 I'll arrive, then I'll call you.

  a) *As soon as I arrive, I'll call you.* (as soon as)

  b) *I won't call you until I arrive.* (until)

2 Justin will know his test scores in July. We'll go on vacation in August.

  a) Justin _____ his test scores _____ on vacation. (before)

  b) _____ on vacation, Justin _____ his test scores. (by the time)

3 The storm will reach the island at about midnight. You'll be asleep by then.

  a) _____ the island, you _____ asleep. (when)

  b) You _____ the storm _____ the island. (before)

4 My classes end soon. Then I'll start this book.

  a) _____ this book _____ my classes _____ . (as soon as)

  b) _____ my classes _____ , _____ this book. (when)

5 I'm going to get to the top of this hill. Then I'm going to sit down and rest—but not before!

  a) _____ , _____ and rest. (as soon as)

  b) I'm _____ the top of this hill. (until)

in case + simple present

5a ★ Match the things to take (1–5) with the reasons (a–e).

Things to take	Why?
1 an MP3 player	a) might be good stores
2 lots of money	b) might want to text my friends
3 some maps	
4 my cell phone	c) might be too quiet for me
5 a few cans of beans	d) might get lost
	e) might not like the food

b ★★ Now write the sentences using *in case* and the simple present.

I'm going to take . . .

1 *an MP3 player in case it's too quiet for me* .

2 _____ .

3 _____ .

4 _____ .

5 _____ .

Consolidation

6 Complete the ads with the correct form of the words from the box.

> • be • by • case • end • if • long • not be
> • not miss • soon • unless • ~~will~~

It's the outdoor rock concert next week. Make sure you have a good time! We can help!

What ^{1} *will* you do ^{2} _____ it rains? If you see black clouds appear in the sky, you'll be worried ^{3} _____ you have our TENT COAT. You can wear it as a coat but, as ^{4} _____ as the music ^{5} _____ and it's time to sleep, you can simply lie down in your own tent!

It's a long festival. You want to take some food in ^{6} _____ you get hungry, but you don't want to carry a lunchbox for two days! There will be food at the festival but you know, ^{7} _____ the time you find the hot dog cart, your favorite band ^{8} _____ in the middle of their last song! Well, as ^{9} _____ as you take a package of MAGIC MEALS, you ^{10} _____ hungry and you ^{11} _____ your favorite band.

MAGIC MEALS
Now in chicken, pizza, and vegetable flavor!

Conditional: *if* clause + past

Affirmative

If I **had** more money, **I would pay** for your pizza.

If Tom **worked** harder, he **might do** better in school.

If I **understood** French, I **could translate** this letter for you.

Negative

If I **lived** closer to school, I **wouldn't have to** get up so early.

If Sara had a computer, she **might not go out** so often.

You **couldn't call** me if you **didn't have** my number.

Questions and short answers

What **would** you **say** if Natalie **asked** you **out**?

If you **were** me, what **would** you **do**?

wish/if only + simple past

Affirmative

I **wish/If only** I **was/were** taller.

I **wish/If only** we **had** more money.

I **wish/If only** I **could** play the piano.

Negative

I **wish/If only** I **wasn't /weren't** so short.

I **wish/If only** I **didn't love** her so much.

I **wish/If only** my little brother **couldn't open** my bedroom door!

Verb + infinitive or gerund

Verb + infinitive

I **want to go** out.

Mark **has decided to study** German.

We **promised not to tell** anyone your secret.

They really **tried not to laugh**.

Verb + gerund

Lisa **can't stand being** late.

We **stopped talking** when the movie started.

Paolo **doesn't mind not getting** the bus.

Our doctor **suggested not eating** anything after eight o'clock.

Verb + infinitive or gerund

I**'ve started to learn/learning** French.

We **like to go/going** into town on Saturdays.

Notes

Conditional: *if* clause + past

Usage

- We use the conditional to talk about unreal or unlikely situations in the present or future.

Form

- There are two parts in a conditional sentence.
  - We use *if + simple past* for the unreal or unlikely condition.
  - We use *would, might, could +* infinitive without *to* for the result.
- The two clauses can be in either order. When the *if* (condition) clause is first, we separate the two clauses with a comma.

be in the conditional

- In informal written or spoken language, we say *If I/he/she/it was . . .*
- In formal written or spoken language, we say *If I/he/she/it were . . .*

wish/if only + simple past

Usage

- We use this verb pattern to talk about present wishes or regrets when the present wish or regret is unlikely or impossible.

Verb + infinitive or gerund

Usage

- We use the infinitive after some verbs, e.g. *agree, decide, encourage, expect, forget, help, hope, manage, offer, promise, refuse, seem, try, want, would like.*
- We use the gerund after some verbs, e.g. *admit, avoid, can't stand, deny, enjoy, finish, give up, keep, miss, not mind, practice, stop, suggest.*
- We can use the gerund or infinitive after some verbs with little or no change in meaning, e.g. *hate, like, love, prefer, start.*
- Some verbs can be followed by an object before the infinitive.
  *My mom encouraged **me** to play tennis.*

Form

- In negative sentences, we add *not* before the infinitive or the gerund.

Grammar Practice

Conditional: *if* clause + past

1 ★ Complete the sentences with the correct form of the verbs in parentheses.

1 If I ___spoke___ (speak) French, I *would move* (move) to France.

2 If I _____ (not have) a little brother, my life _____ (may be) easier.

3 I _____ (not want) to live at home if I _____ (be) a student.

4 If you _____ (not spend) so much time on your computer, you _____ (may read) more.

5 If you _____ (be) an actor, _____ (you want) to live in Hollywood?

2 ★★ Write conditional sentences using the information.

1 If I knew how to drive . . .

a) Dad lend me his car (maybe)

   Dad might lend me his car.

b) I buy a new car (no)

   I wouldn't buy a new car.

c) take my friends to the beach (possible)

   I could take my friends to the beach.

2 If I had a part-time job . . .

a) have time to do all my homework (no)

   _____

b) meet some cool people (maybe)

   _____

c) save up money for the summer (possible)

   _____

3 If I had a girlfriend . . .

a) go to parties with her (possible)

   _____

b) have time for my friends (maybe not)

   _____

c) be happy (yes!)

   _____

wish/if only + simple past

3 ★ Write sentences using the cues. Use *wish* or *if only* and the simple past.

1 only / we / have / a map

   If only we had a map.

2 wish / I not have / so much homework to do

   _____

3 only / I / not be / so shy

   _____

4 wish / the water / not be / so cold

   _____

4 ★★ Complete the sentences so that they mean the same as the originals.

1 I have a younger brother. I want a sister!

If _____*only I had*_____ a sister.

___*I wish I didn't have*___ a younger brother.

2 I live in a boring part of town. I want to live near my friends.

I _____ a boring part of town.

If _____ my friends.

3 I don't understand French. My teacher talks too quickly.

I _____ so quickly.

If _____ French.

4 My dad doesn't like my boyfriend. I can't see him during the week.

If _____ my boyfriend.

I _____ during the week.

Verb + infinitive or gerund

5 ★ Complete the sentences with the infinitive or gerund (-ing) form of the verbs in parentheses.

1 Pete denied ___*going*___ (go) to the party.

2 Pete wanted ___*to go*___ (go) to the party.

3 Amy avoided _____ (talk) to Leo.

4 I'm still trying _____ (do) my homework.

5 I don't enjoy _____ (read) poetry.

6 Jason promised not _____ (borrow) my CDs.

6 ★★ Look at the information and complete the sentences with the infinitive or gerund (-ing) form of the verbs.

1 **Jake:** I'm going fishing.

Jake has decided ___*to go fishing*___ .

2 **Maria:** Oh, please, can I have a party?

Maria wants _____ .

3 **Clyde:** I'm not going to ski any more.

Clyde has given up _____ .

4 **Ellie:** Oh, no. I didn't lock the door.

Ellie forgot _____ .

5 **Jess:** Soccer on TV is so boring.

Jess can't stand _____ .

Consolidation

7 Circle the correct answers.

Greg: Can I borrow your cell phone?

Nick: Sure. It's not very good. I wish I **1** ____ a better one.

Greg: Why?

Nick: If I had a better cell phone, I **2** ____ photos.

Greg: What do you want **3** ____ photos of?

Nick: I don't know. Anything. I enjoy **4** ____ photos but I always forget **5** ____ batteries in my camera.

Greg: Uh, Nick. Your phone isn't working. The batteries are dead!

1 a) have   b) would have   c) had

2 a) took   b) could take   c) will take

3 a) to take   b) taking   c) take

4 a) take   b) to take   c) taking

5 a) putting   b) put   c) to put

Ruth: I wish I **6** ____ travel in time.

Nicola: Where **7** ____ go back to?

Ruth: 3:15 on Saturday afternoon.

Nicola: Why?

Ruth: I lost my MP3 player somewhere. If I **8** ____ back in time, I might find out what happened to it.

Nicola: You'd have to keep **9** ____ back in time.

Ruth: Why?

Nicola: You're always losing things! You should stop **10** ____ about time travel and concentrate on what you're doing.

6 a) would   b) could   c) might

7 a) did you   b) you would c) would you

8 a) went   b) go   c) would go

9 a) go   b) to go   c) going

10 a) dreaming b) dream   c) to dream

Reported statements and questions

Statements
Direct statement / **Reported statement**

"I **play** video games every day." / He **said that he played** video games every day.

"I**'m texting** my friend." / Mary **said that she was texting** her friend.

"We **went** to the movies **last night.**" / They **said that they had gone** to the movies **the previous night.**

"I**'ll try** to arrive by eight o'clock." / She **told us that she would try** to arrive by eight o'clock.

"I **can meet** you after school." / He **said he could meet** us after school.

Wh- questions
Direct question / **Reported question**

"**What do** you **want**?" / She **asked him what he wanted.**

"**Where are** you **going**?" / He **asked me where I was going.**

"**When will** you **be** ready?" / She **asked him when he would be** ready.

"**When can** we **leave**?" / He **asked us when we could leave.**

Yes/No questions
Direct question / **Reported question**

"**Do** you ever **use** chat sites?" / He **asked me if/whether** I ever **used** chat sites.

"**Can** Steve **swim**?" / She **asked us if/whether** Steve **could swim.**

"**Will** you **tell** her tomorrow?" / He **asked me if/whether I would tell** her **the next day.**

Notes
Reported statements and questions
Usage
- We use reported speech to report what someone has said. We use *say* or *tell* in statements and *ask* in questions.

Form
- When we change a direct statement or question to a reported one we make some changes to the structure.
  - We move the tense "back".
    simple present → simple past
    present continuous → past continuous
    simple past → past perfect
    present perfect → past perfect
    will/can/may → would/could/might
  - We usually change pronouns.
    "*We're from London.*" → They said (that) *they* were from London.
  - We usually change possessive adjectives.
    "*That's my T-shirt.*" → She said (that) it was *her* T-shirt.
  - We also change time and place references.
    here → *there*
    this → *that*
    these → *those*
    today → *that day*
    yesterday → *the previous day/day before*
    tomorrow → *the next/following day*
- If we are reporting something immediate, we don't need to change the tense or other words.
  Tim's on the phone. He **says he'll meet** *us at six o'clock.*
- In reported questions, the word order is the same as a statement.
- We don't use the auxiliary *do/did*. We write other auxiliaries after the object.
- In *Wh-* questions, we use *asked* + (object) + question word + subject + verb.
- In *Yes/No* questions, we use *asked* + (object) + *if/whether* + subject + verb.
- We don't write a question mark at the end of a reported question.

Reporting verbs

Followed by infinitive

She **told us not to talk** during the test.

They **asked us to leave**.

He **refused to eat** his dinner.

Followed by gerund (*-ing* form)

Sara **admitted losing** my book.

I **suggested going** to the movies.

Chris **apologized** for **waking** us **up**.

Followed by *that* and a clause

Harry **explained that** he had missed the bus.

Seth **denied that** he had broken the phone.

Nick **suggested that** we go home.

Subordinating conjunctions that show contrast; *although, in spite of/ despite, however, on the other hand*

Although we were tired, we finished our work.

In spite of being tired, we finished our work.

Despite being tired, we finished our work.

We'd had a long day and we were tired. **However,** we finished our work before we went to bed.

We'd had a long day and we wanted to stop work. **On the other hand,** we wanted to finish before we went to bed.

Notes

Reporting verbs

Form

There are different reporting verb forms.

- With verbs such as *agree, ask, encourage, invite, order, persuade, promise, refuse,* and *tell,* we use the structure reporting verb + *(not)* + *to* + infinitive.
- With verbs such as *admit, apologize, carry on, deny, keep,* and *suggest,* we use the structure reporting verb + *(not)* + gerund (*-ing* form). Some verbs are followed by a preposition, e.g. *apologize for.*
- With verbs such as *admit, complain, deny, explain,* and *suggest,* we use the structure reporting verb + *that* + clause.
- Some reporting verbs have more than one possible structure with no change in meaning.
  She **denied being** responsible.
  She **denied that she was** responsible.

Subordinating conjunctions that show contrast; *although, in spite of/despite, however, on the other hand*

Usage

- We use these words and phrases to contrast two ideas.

Form

- *Although* can come at the beginning of a sentence or between the two ideas.
- *Despite* and *in spite of* are followed by the gerund (*-ing* form) of the verb.
- We usually start a second sentence which contrasts with the first with *however* or *on the other hand.*

Grammar Practice

Reported statements and questions

1 ★ Match the people (a–d) with the reported statements and questions (1–4).

a) **Kate:** What are you going to do tomorrow?

b) ~~Sam:~~ I don't think I'll send any e-mails today.

c) **Beth:** These are my video games.

d) **Rob:** Did you use your computer yesterday?

1 _Sam_ said that he didn't think he would send any e-mails that day.

2 _____ asked if I had used my computer the previous day.

3 _____ said that those were her video games.

4 _____ asked what we were going to do the following day.

2 ★★ Report the conversations.

1 **Seth:** What's your name?

  Ben: My name's Ben.

  Seth asked Ben _____ _what his name was_ _____.

  Ben said that _____ _his name was Ben_ _____.

2 **Tom:** What do you want to do?

  Claire: I don't know. Is there anything good at the movie theater?

  Tom asked Claire _____.

  She said that _____

  and she asked _____.

3 **Neil:** Where've you been?

  Matt: I went to the library to get a book for my project.

  Neil asked Matt _____.

  Matt told Neil that _____.

4 **Sam:** Can I stay out until ten o'clock?

  Mom: Yes, you can. I'll pick you up in the car.

  Sam asked his mom _____.

  His mom said that _____ and that she

  _____.

Reporting verbs

3 ★ Circle the correct answers.

1 Lisa admitted *to copy / (copying)* her homework from her brother.

2 Mrs. Li told us *not to / to not* open our books yet.

3 I promised *helping / to help* my mom with the shopping.

4 Did you agree *to go / going* to Michelle's party?

5 Why did you suggest *watching / to watch* this movie? It's awful.

6 Mark complained to the waiter that his fork *is / was* dirty.

7 Damian apologized *for / with* being rude.

4 ★★ Make reported speech sentences.

1 for / our / tests / teacher / not / Our / grading / apologized

  Our teacher apologized for not grading our tests.

2 properly / work / new / that / my / I / complained / computer / didn't

  _____

  _____

3 My / had / that / my / read / diary / sister / denied / she

  _____

  _____

4 us / to / home / Nick's dad / offered / drive

  _____

  _____

5 the party / we / Meg / her / why / to / invited / hadn't / us / asked

  _____

  _____

6 lying / Wayne / his / about / new / admitted / computer

  _____

  _____

5 ★★ Match the functions (a–e) with the sentences (1–5) and then rewrite them in reported speech. Make any changes necessary.

> a) an apology   b) a complaint   c) an invitation
> d) a suggestion   ~~e) a promise~~

1 "I will work harder next year." (Kelly to her mom)

☐ e *Kelly promised to work harder the*
following year.

2 "Would you like to come to my brother's
eighteenth birthday party?" (Harry to me)

☐ _____

_____

3 "I'm sorry I got home late last night." (Me to my
parents)

☐ _____

_____

4 "Why don't we go to the mall on Saturday."
(Debbie to me)

☐ _____

_____

5 "Your writing is so bad that I can't read it." (Mrs.
Clark to Tom)

☐ _____

_____

Subordinating conjunctions that show contrast

6 ★★ Write the sentence below in four
different ways using the words in parentheses.

"I knew the answers to the questions but I made
some stupid mistakes."

1 (although) *Although I knew the answers to the*
questions, I made some stupid mistakes.

2 (however) _____

_____

3 (in spite of) _____

_____

4 (despite) _____

_____

Consolidation

7 Complete the article with the correct form of
the words from the box.

> • ~~although~~ • be • be • despite • have • love
> • not know • spite • want

1 ___*Although*___ Daniel Radcliffe was only twelve
when the first *Harry Potter* movie came out, it
wasn't his first movie. He had already acted with
Pierce Brosnan in *The Tailor of Panama* earlier that
year. He also appeared in the Australian movie
December Boys, **2** _____ not being Australian.

In interviews, Daniel has talked about a wide range
of topics.

Music: He said that his favorite band **3** _____
the American group, *The Hold Steady*. He also likes
the *Libertines* and said that he **4** _____ them
to sing "Happy Birthday" to him one year.

Sports: Daniel told interviewers that he
5 _____ to play cricket and that, once, he
6 _____ a strange dream in which one of the
England cricketers was chasing him with his bat.

Girls: Daniel admitted **7** _____ very nervous
around girls. He said that he **8** _____ what to
say to them.

Harry Potter: Daniel said that, in **9** _____ of
spending nine years of his life making *Harry Potter*
movies, he never got bored and he would miss
playing the part.

---

so + adjective/adverb (that) . . . , such a/an + adjective + noun (that) . . . , so many/much + noun (that) . . . , Verb + so much (that) . . .

so + adjective/adverb (that) . . .

I was **so tired that** I fell asleep on the bus.

Mr. Finch speaks **so quickly that** I can't understand anything he says.

such a/an + adjective + noun (that) . . .

St. Ives is **such a beautiful town that** I want to live there.

I had **such an awful headache that** I couldn't see the computer.

so many/much + noun (that) . . .

There are **so many delicious things** on the menu **that** I don't know what to choose.

We spent **so much time** in the museum **that** we didn't have time for dinner.

Verb + so much (that) . . .

I **ate so much that** I felt sick.

Notes

so + adjective/adverb (that) . . . , such a/an + adjective + noun (that) . . . , so many/much + noun (that) . . . , Verb + so much (that) . . .

Usage

- We use *so* to emphasize adjectives and adverbs.
- We use *such a/an* to emphasize adjectives.
- We use *so many* with plural count nouns.
  *There were **so many T-shirts that** I didn't know which one to choose.*
- We use *so much* with noncount nouns.
  *I had **so much luggage that** I couldn't carry it all.*
- We use *so* + adjective, *such a/an* + adjective + noun, *so many/much* + noun and verb + *so much* to show cause and effect.
  The sea was cold. (simple fact)
  *The sea was **so cold that** we couldn't swim.* (cause: the sea was so cold; effect: we couldn't swim)

Common mistakes

~~Our teacher was too angry that he shouted at us.~~ ✗

Our teacher was so angry that he shouted at us. ✓

~~We had such a good time than we didn't want to leave.~~ ✗

We had such a good time that we didn't want to leave. ✓

used to/be used to/get used to

used to
Affirmative
I **used to live** in Seattle.
Negative
I **didn't use to live** in Seattle.
Questions and short answers
Did you **use to** be a singer?   Yes, I **did**. No, I **didn't**.

be used to
Affirmative
I**'m used to being** on my own.
Negative
Maria **isn't used to working** at home.
Questions and short answers
Are you **used to wearing** a uniform? Yes, I **am**. No, I**'m not**.

get used to
Affirmative
Tom**'s getting used to having** a baby brother.
Negative
Jess **is getting used to not having** a computer.
Questions and short answers
Is Jack **getting used to living** in the U.S.?
Yes, he **is**. No, he **isn't**.

be able to

Affirmative
I **was able to** buy a new phone.
She **was able to** play the piano when she was five.
We**'ll be able to** leave soon.
Negative
Beth **wasn't able to** finish her homework.
She**'s never been able to** play the piano.
You **won't be able to** do this puzzle.
Questions and short answers
Were you **able to** answer all the questions?
Yes, I **was**. No, I **wasn't**.
Will Harry **be able to** come to the party?
Yes, he **will**. No, he **won't**.

Notes

used to/be used to/get used to
Usage
- We use *used to* + infinitive to talk about past habits or states that are not true now.
- We use *be used to* + gerund (*-ing* form) to talk about habits in the present.
- We use *get used to* + gerund (*-ing* form) to talk about new experiences we are learning about.

Form
used to
- The form is the same for all persons.
- In affirmative sentences, we use *used to* + infinitive without *to*.
- In negative sentences, we use *didn't* + *use to* + infinitive without *to*.
- In questions, we use *did* + subject + *use to* + infinitive without *to*.
- Do not confuse *used to* for past habits with the verb *to use*.
  He **used to travel** by bus everywhere. (= past habit)
  He *used a bus to travel to the concert.* (= made use of)

be used to/get used to
- In affirmative sentences, we use *be* + *used to* + gerund (*-ing* form) or *get* + *used to* + gerund.
- In negative sentences, we add *not*.
- We add *not* after the verb *to be* to show that we are not used to something.
- We add *not* before the gerund to show that we are used to a negative situation.
- In questions, we use *be* + subject + *used to* + gerund or *get* + subject + *used to* + gerund.

Common mistakes
~~Which school did you used to go to?~~ ✗
Which school did you use to go to? ✓
~~I'm used to have more free time.~~ ✗
I'm used to having more free time. ✓

be able to
Usage
- We use *be able to* to talk about what happened in a particular situation.

so + adjective/adverb (that) . . . , such a/an + adjective + noun (that) . . . , so many/much + noun (that) . . . , Verb + so much (that) . . .

1 ★ Complete the sentences with so or such.

1 I'm _____ *so* _____ angry with my brother.

2 How can you be _____ calm?

3 This is _____ a depressing song that it makes me want to cry.

4 We had _____ a great time on vacation.

5 I've never felt _____ lonely before.

2 ★★ Write sentences with so or such.

1 It was / boring book / I couldn't finish it
   It was such a boring book that I couldn't finish it.

2 Lisa / cheerful person / makes us all feel happy

   _____

3 The book / confusing / I didn't understand anything

   _____

4 This game / exciting / I play it all the time

   _____

used to/be used to/get used to

3 ★ Complete the sentences with the correct form of used to + gerund (-ing form).

It's been a strange two months at my new school but I'm slowly getting used to it.

Things I'm used to now
1 I have homework every day.
2 I'm the youngest student in the school.

Things I'm getting used to
3 I eat school lunches.
4 I go to school by bus.

Things I'm still not used to
5 I sit next to a girl in class!

1 ___*I'm used to having*___ homework every day.

2 _____ the youngest student in the school.

3 _____ school lunches.

4 _____ to school by bus.

5 _____ next to a girl.

4 ★★ Use the information to say what Jane is used to (✓), isn't used to (✗), and is getting used to (≈) in her new weekend job.

1 She starts work early. (✓)
   Jane is used to starting work early.

2 She cleans the toilets. (✗)

   _____

3 She serves customers. (≈)

   _____

4 She does all her homework on Sundays. (≈)

   _____

5 She has money in her pocket. (✓)

   _____

6 Her boss shouts at her. (✗)

   _____

be able to

5 ★ Complete the sentences with the correct form of *be able to*.

1 My sister couldn't talk until she was three.

My sister _wasn't able to talk_ until she was three.

2 I'm sorry. It's impossible for me to see you tomorrow.

I'm sorry. I _____ you tomorrow.

3 I can't meet my friends next weekend.

I _____ my friends next weekend.

4 Did you manage to contact Paul last night?

_____ Paul last night?

5 Is it possible for you to help me tomorrow?

_____ me tomorrow?

6 My mom has never managed to finish a Sudoku puzzle.

My mom _____ a Sudoku puzzle.

6 ★★ Look at the information and write sentences using the correct form of *be able to*.

Past ability

1 Walking – age 2

2 Riding a bike – age 6

Future ability

3 Leaving home – age 16

4 Learning to drive – age 17

Abilities he's never had

5 Keeping his room neat

6 Remembering his school books

Ben, age 15

1 _Ben was able to walk when he was two._

2 _____

3 _____

4 _____

5 _____

6 _____

Consolidation

7 Circle the correct answers.

"We used **1** ____ the best goalie in the country. He was **2** ____ good goalie that no one was **3** ____ score against us. Now we have to get used **4** ____ the worst goalie!"

1 a) have   b) having   c) to have

2 a) so   b) such a   c) such

3 a) used to   b) able to   c) could

4 a) to having   b) to have   c) have

"I haven't gotten used **5** ____ famous yet. There are **6** ____ photographers here."

"I know. The only person who used **7** ____ our picture was our mom."

5 a) to be   b) being   c) to being

6 a) so much   b) such   c) so many

7 a) to take   b) to taking   c) take

"We're raising **8** ____ money!"

"I know. I **9** ____ to seeing **10** ____ people at one of our charity events."

8 a) so much   b) so many   c) such

9 a) 'm not used   b) didn't use   c) won't be able

10 a) so much   b) such a lot   c) so many

Causative *have*

I **had** my bike **fixed** last week.
She**'s having** her hair **washed** right now.
We **have never had** our roof **repaired**.
They**'re going to have** their photo **taken** tomorrow.
I **need to have** my teeth **checked**.

Clauses of purpose: *to, in order (not) to, so that*

We went to the bank **to/in order to** get some money.
I get up early every day **in order not to** be late for school.
We bought tickets for the concert on the Internet **so that** we wouldn't have to wait on line.
My dad always walks to work **so that** he gets some exercise every day.

look, seem, sound, feel, taste, smell + adjective /like/as if

look, seem, sound, feel, taste, smell + adjective

That pizza **looks delicious**.
Sara **seemed excited** today.
My phone **sounds strange**.
I **feel ill**.
This food **tastes delicious**.
This milk **smells disgusting**.

look, seem, sound, feel, taste, smell + like

Mark **looks like** his dad.
That **seems like** a good idea.
This band **sounds like** U2.
This **feels like** silk but it isn't.
These oranges **taste like** lemons.
This **smells like** Chinese food.

look, seem, sound, feel, taste, smell + as if

Tom **looks as if** he's been awake all night.
It **seems as if** we've gone the wrong way.
You **sound as if** you have a cold.
This sweater **feels as if** it's made of wool.
This chicken **tastes as if** it hasn't been cooked properly.
These sneakers **smell as if** they need to be washed!

Notes
Causative *have*
Usage
- We use causative *have* to talk about things we have arranged for other people to do for us.
  I **had** my hair **cut**. (The hairdresser cut it.)

Form
- We use *have* + noun + past participle. We change the tense of the structure by changing the tense of the verb *have*.
- The past participle always comes after the object.

Common mistakes
She's having her eyes testing now. ✗
She's having her eyes tested now. ✓
I had repaired my TV. ✗
I had my TV repaired. ✓

Clauses of purpose: *to, in order (not) to, so that*
Usage
- We use clauses of purpose to say why we do something.
- *in order to* is more formal.

Form
- *to* and *in order (not) to* are followed by the infinitive; *so that* is followed by a clause with a subject.

look, seem, sound, feel, taste, smell + adjective /like/as if
Usage
- We use these structures to compare one thing with another or make judgments about things based on our senses.

Form
- When we use an adjective only to make our judgments, we use the verb and adjective without *like* or *as if*.
- When we compare something to another noun, we use verb + *like* + noun.
- When we use a clause to make our judgments, we use verb + *as if* + clause.

Common mistakes
He looks like tired. ✗
He looks tired. ✓

Grammar Practice

Causative *have*

1 ★ Complete the sentences with the correct form of the verbs in parentheses.

1 I _had_ (have) my bike _fixed_ (fix) yesterday.

2 I'm going _____ (have) my computer _____ (check) tomorrow.

3 Erin _____ (have) her hair _____ (wash) today.

4 My mom wants my dad _____ (have) his heart _____ (examine).

5 My sister needs _____ (have) her pants _____ (shorten).

6 My dad often _____ (have) his car _____ (clean) at the gas station.

7 Have you ever _____ (have) your eyes _____ (test)?

2 ★★ Rewrite the sentences using causative *have*.

1 A man painted our living room.
We _had our living room painted_ .

2 Someone fixed my bike for me.
I _____ .

3 Has anyone ever serviced your brother's motorcycle?
Has your brother ever _____ _____ ?

4 Has someone cut your hair?
Have _____ ?

5 The dentist is going to take one of my teeth out.
I'm _____ .

6 I need someone to replace my front tire.
I need _____ .

7 You'd better ask someone to clean your jacket before the concert.
You'd better _____ _____ .

Clauses of purpose: *to, in order (not) to, so that*

3 ★ Use the cues to complete the sentences.
Why does our teacher makes us do projects?

1 – lessons not boring
. . . so _____ that the lessons aren't _____ boring.

2 – makes us work
. . . in _____ us work.

3 – she can rest!
. . . so _____ rest!

4 – we don't do the same thing every day
. . . in _____
the same thing every day.

4 ★★ Combine the sentences using the words in parentheses.

1 I download the news to my phone. I don't want to miss anything important. (in order not to)
I download the news to my phone *in order not to miss anything important* .

2 I'm staying at home today. I want to finish my homework. (so that)
I'm staying at home today _____
_____ .

3 I go to the gym twice a week. I want to get in shape. (in order to)
I go to the gym _____
_____ .

4 Ben plays basketball every day after school. He wants to get onto the school team. (in order to)
Ben _____
_____ .

5 I wrote my friend's number down. I didn't want to forget it. (in order not to)
I wrote _____
_____ .

look, seem, sound, feel, taste, smell + adjective /like/as if

5 ★ Write sentences using the cues.

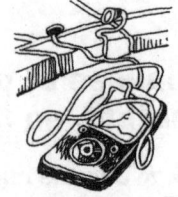

There's something wrong with my MP3 player.

1 It / look / it / has been / dropped on the ground

  It looks as if it's been dropped on the ground.

2 The music / sound / really strange

You must have been busy preparing this dinner.

3 It / smell / delicious

_____

4 You / not look / you have been cooking for hours

_____

6 ★★ Complete the sentences with the correct form of *look, sound, feel, taste, smell,* and any other words necessary.

1 They *look* cool, they *sound*

great, but they  *smell* awful!

2 It  ✗ _____ chicken, it

 ✗ _____ chicken, and it

✗ _____ chicken . . . because

there's no chicken in it at all!

3 It 👁 👁 _____ nice and soft but it

✗ _____ nice and soft and the

girl 👁 👁 ✗ _____ happy!

Consolidation

7 Complete the conversation with the correct form of the words from the box.

> • cut • have (x2) • if • like • ̶l̶o̶o̶k̶e̶d̶ • not
> • order • so • sounded • taken

Liam: Did you see Jamie today?

Charles: Yes, his hair **1** *looked* awful. He should

    2 _____ it **3** _____. It's too long.

Liam: About a month ago he got a tattoo on his

    forehead. He grows his hair long

    4 _____ that no one will see it.

Charles: A tattoo on his forehead! Wait a minute,

    you're joking, aren't you?

Liam: Yes, but you believed me for a minute.

Charles: Well, you **5** _____ as **6** _____ you

    were telling the truth. So, why is his hair so

    long?

Liam: He grows it in **7** _____ to look more

    8 _____ a TV star. Lots of people think

    he's Zac Ephron. When I saw him, he was

    9 _____ his photo **10** _____ by some

    paparazzi.

Charles: That's another joke, right?

Liam: No, it's true. Well, it was only Ted Rogers

    from the local paper, but he really thought

    Jamie was a TV star. I had to leave in order

    11 _____ to laugh. Hey, do you think I

    look like Mitchel Musso?

Charles: You look more like Mickey Mouse. ☺

Grammar Summary

should have/ought to have

Affirmative

I/You/He/She/It/We/They **should have/ought to have tried** harder.

I/You/He/She/It/We/They **should have/ought to have known** what would happen.

Negative

I/You/He/She/It/We/They **shouldn't have/oughtn't (ought not) to have been** so rude.

I/You/He/She/It/We/They **shouldn't have/oughtn't to have shouted**.

must/can't/might/could for deductions in the present

Certainty

I/You/He/She/It/We/They **must be dreaming**.

It **must be** his day off work.

I/You/He/She/It/We/They **couldn't speak** French when I/You/He/She/It/They was/were young.

I/You/He/She/It/We/They **can't go** to this school.

Possibility

The burglar **might not have gone** upstairs.

You **might win** that competition.

We **could be** the youngest people here.

Notes

should have/ought to have

Usage

- We use *should have* or *ought to have* to
  - talk about regrets about our own past actions.

    I **shouldn't have worn** that dress.
  - criticize or give advice about other people's past actions.

    You **should have finished** that an hour ago. You **should have seen** the movie when it was at the theater. It was great.

Form

- We use *should/ought to* + *have* + past participle.
- *Oughtn't* (*ought not*) is very formal and rarely used.

Common mistakes

~~You shouldn't have went to bed so late.~~ ✗

You shouldn't have gone to bed so late. ✓

~~He ought have worked harder.~~ ✗

He ought to have worked harder. ✓

must/can't/might/could for deductions in the present

Usage

- We use *must* when we are very sure something is true, although we don't know for a fact.

  He **must be** the new student.
  (I'm sure but I don't know for a fact.)
- We use *can't* when we are sure that something is not possible, although we don't know for a fact.

  The Loch Ness Monster **can't** really **exist**.
  (I'm sure of this but I don't know for a fact.)
- We use *might* or *could* when something is possible but we are not very sure.

  They **might/could be stuck** in traffic.
  (It is a possibility but I'm not sure this is the reason they are late.)

Form

- We use *must/can't/might/could* + infinitive without *to*.

must have/can't have/might have/could have for deductions in the past

Certainty
I/You/He/She/It/We/They **must have gone** the wrong way.
I/You/He/She/It/We/They **can't have locked** the door.

Possibility
I/You/He/She/It/We/They **might have called** the wrong number.
I/You/He/She/It/We/They **might not have heard** the phone.

Notes

must have/can't have/might have/could have for deductions in the past

Usage
- We use *must have* when we are very sure something about the past is true, although we don't know for a fact.
  *He **must have enjoyed** the movie.*
  (I'm sure but I don't know for a fact.)
- We use *can't have* when we are sure that something didn't happen in the past, although we don't know this for a fact.
  *Max **can't have robbed** the bank.*
  (I'm sure of this but I don't know for a fact.)
- We use *might have/could have* when something about the past is possible but we are not very sure that it happened.
  *She **might have/could have forgotten** her phone.*
  (It is a possibility but I'm not sure this is the reason she hasn't called me.)

Form
- We use *must have/can't have/might have/could have* + past participle.

Common mistakes
They must have went home. ✗
They must have gone home. ✓
The burglar can have climbed through the window. ✗
The burglar could have climbed through the window. ✓

Grammar Practice

should have/ought to have

1 ★ **Put the words in the correct order. Then match the sentences (1–5) with the problems (a–e).**

1 bed / should / earlier / have / to / You / gone
You should have gone to bed earlier.

2 You / worked / harder / have / should

_____

3 ought / safe / somewhere / put / You / to / them / have

_____

4 to / You / your / ought / have / dinner / finished

_____

5 your / before / e-mail / shouldn't / checked / You / have / breakfast

_____

a) I'm tired.   *1*
b) I'm hungry.   _____
c) I'm late for school. _____
d) I failed my test.   _____
e) I can't find my keys. _____

2 ★★ **Rewrite B's replies using the verbs in parentheses.**

1 A: My MP3 player is broken.

   B: You should have been more careful with it. (ought to)

   You ought to have been more careful with it.

2 A: We were really worried when we realized that Phil wasn't with us.

   B: He shouldn't have gone home without telling anyone. (ought not to)

   He _____

3 A: I was only ten minutes late but Tom had already gone home.

   B: He ought to have waited for longer than ten minutes. (should)

   Tom _____

4 A: I didn't have a bus ticket and now I have to pay $15.

   B: You ought not to have gotten on the bus without a ticket. (shouldn't)

   You _____

5 A: Where are we? This isn't Emma's house.

   B: We should have turned left at the post office, not right. (shouldn't)

   We _____,

   we should have turned left.

must/can't/might/could for deductions in the present

3 ★★ **Read the conversations and complete the sentences. Use *must*, *can't*, or *might*, or *could* and a verb.**

Sue: Karen's crying.
Laura: Is she upset?
Sue: I'm sure she is. That's why people cry!
Laura: Do you think she's lost?
Sue: No way! She's been here for three years.
Laura: Do you think she's having problems with Dave?
Sue: It's possible. They're always arguing.

1 Karen ____*must be*____ upset.

2 Karen _____ lost.

3 Karen _____ having problems with Dave.

Cathy: Who's that boy? He's looking at us strangely.
Max: That's the new student. He's from Italy.
Cathy: Do you think he's lost?
Max: It's possible! I'll go and ask him.
Cathy: Does he speak English?
Max: I'm sure he does. His mom's American.
Cathy: Do you think he likes living here in Chicago?
Max: No way! Chicago in February must be really cold compared to Italy.

4 The boy _____ lost.

5 The boy _____ English.

6 The boy _____ living in Chicago.

4 ★★ Write sentences using *must, can't, might,* or *could*. Use the information in parentheses to help you decide which to use.

1 My dad's at home. (It's possible.)

   My dad might/could be at home.

2 It's time for bed. (I'm sure it's not true.)

   _____

3 You have the wrong books. (I'm sure it's true.)

   _____

4 Paul is Sandra's boyfriend. (I'm sure it isn't true.)

   _____

5 Your sister likes Beyoncé. (I'm sure it's true.)

   _____

6 We're in the wrong room. (It's possible.)

   _____

must have/can't have/might have/ could have for deductions in the past

5 ★ Read Seb's story and then complete his ideas using the verbs in parentheses.

> Yesterday, as I was walking home from work, I saw two men running out of the bank. They weren't carrying anything but they kept looking behind them. A few minutes later, two police cars raced past. Here's what I think.

1 The two men *must have done* something wrong. (must do)

2 They _____ to rob the bank. (might try)

3 They _____ dangerous. (might be)

4 They _____ any money. (can't steal)

5 Something _____ wrong. (must go)

6 The people in the bank _____ frightened. (must be)

7 Someone in the bank _____ the police. (might call)

8 The police _____ the two men later. (might catch)

9 Or the two men _____ away. (might get away)

Consolidation

6 Read the conversation and circle the correct answers.

Sam: Where's Mike? He **1** ____ here by now.

Hannah: He **2** ____ on the bus. Why don't you call him?

Sam: I tried but he didn't answer. He **3** ____ his phone at home.

Hannah: He **4** ____ it. He always has it.

Sam: He **5** ____ asleep on the bus. He was very tired today.

Hannah: Yes, he **6** ____ to bed late last night.

Sam: Yes, he was probably updating his website again. Oh, . . . wait a minute. That's my phone. It **7** ____ him. Hello.

Mike: Hi. It's Mike. Sorry, I'm late. I was talking to Mr. Clements about my grades. That's why I didn't answer my phone. I **8** ____ you earlier. Anyway, I'm on the bus now and I'll be there in about twenty minutes.

Sam: OK. We'll be in the café. It **9** ____ difficult to get a table if we don't hurry.

1 a) must have been   (b) should have been)
   c) can't have been

2 a) could be   b) can't be   c) shouldn't have been

3 a) might leave   b) should have left
   c) must have left

4 a) can't have forgotten   b) might have forgotten
   c) must have forgotten

5 a) could fall   b) can't have fallen
   c) might have fallen

6 a) must go   b) should have gone
   c) must have gone

7 a) must have been   b) must be
   c) ought to have been

8 a) ought to have called   b) can't have called
   c) must have called

9 a) must be   b) can't be   c) could be

The passive: simple present, simple past, present perfect, past perfect

Simple present

Affirmative
I **am driven** to school (by my parents).
You/We/They **are given** lots of homework (by the teacher).
He/She/It **is photographed** by the paparazzi every week.

Negative
Newspapers **aren't sold** here. He/She/It **isn't told** what to do.

Questions and short answers
Is this movie **shown** on satellite TV? Yes, it **is**. No, it **isn't**.
Are actors **paid** too much? Yes, they **are**. No, they **aren't**.

Simple past

Affirmative
I/He/She/It **was introduced** to all the guests.
You/We/They **were shown** a movie.

Negative
I/He/She/It **wasn't allowed** to use a camera.
You/We/They **weren't given** the location.

Questions and short answers
Was she **accused** of a crime? Yes, she **was**. No, she **wasn't**.
Were they **followed**? Yes, they **were**. No, they **weren't**.

Present perfect

Affirmative
I/You/We/They **have been told** to clean up the mess.
He/She/It **has been sentenced** to three years in prison.

Negative
I/You/We/They **haven't been followed** by the paparazzi before.
He/She/It **hasn't been seen** in public for two months.

Questions and short answers
Have I **been told** the truth? Yes, you **have**. No, you **haven't**.
Has he **been given** the facts? Yes, he **has**. No, he **hasn't**.

Past perfect

Affirmative
I/You/He/She/It/We/They **had been recognized**.

Negative
I/You/He/She/It/We/They **hadn't been arrested** before.

Questions and short answers
Had I/you/he/she/it/we/they **been informed**?
Yes/No, I/you/he/she/it/we/they **had/hadn't**.

Notes

The passive: simple present, simple past, present perfect, past perfect

Usage
- We use the passive to say what is, was, or has been done to a person.
- We use the passive when
  - we don't know the subject.
    *Our house **was robbed**.*
    (Someone robbed our house.)
  - the action or the object is more important than the subject.
    *We **were leaving** the school when we **were told** to be quiet. (We were leaving the school when Mr. Smith told us to be quiet.)*
  - when we want to avoid mentioning who did something.
    *Mistakes **have been made** but now it's OK. (We've made some mistakes but now it's OK.)*

Form
- We form the simple present and simple past passive with the correct form of *to be* + the past participle of the verb.
  Active: *Our teacher **gives us** homework every day.*
  Passive: *We **are given** homework every day.*
  Active: *The judge **sentenced** the criminal to ten years in prison.*
  Passive: *The criminal **was sentenced** to ten years in prison.*
- If it is important to say who or what the agent (= subject) is/was, we use *by*.
  *We **are given** homework every day by our teacher.*
  *The burglar **was sentenced** by the judge.*
- We form the present perfect and past perfect passive by using *has been/have been* or *had been* + past participle.
  Active: *Someone **has given** me a gift.*
  Passive: *I've **been given** a gift.*
  Active: *It was the first time someone **had recognized** me in the street.*
  Passive: *It was the first time I **had been recognized** in the street.*

The passive: present continuous, past continuous, and simple future

Present continuous

Affirmative

I **am being followed**. You/We/They **are being arrested**.
He/She/It **is being robbed**.

Negative

I **am not being sent** home. You/We/They **are not being arrested**.
He/She/It **isn't being chased** by a robber.

Questions and short answers

Am I being asked a question? Yes, you **are**. No, you **aren't**.
Are you **being questioned**? Yes I am. No, I'm not.
Is he **being filmed** in Seattle? Yes, he **is**. No, he **isn't**.

Past continuous

Affirmative

I/He/She/It **was being taken** to the hospital.
You/We/They **were being interviewed** by a reporter.

Negative

I/He/She/It **wasn't being paid** for the photographs.
You/We/They **weren't being interviewed** by a reporter.

Questions and short answers

Was he **being told** what to do? Yes, he **was**. No, he **wasn't**.
Were they **being interviewed**? Yes, they **were**. No, they **weren't**.

Future simple

Affirmative

I/You/He/She/It/We/They **will be given** a part in the new show.

Negative

I/You/He/She/It/We/They **won't be seen** in the new show.

Questions and short answers

Will we **be shown** the photographs? Yes, you **will**. No, you **won't**.

The passive: modals, gerund (-*ing* form), and infinitive

Modals

I/You/He/She/It/We/They **can/should/must/ought to be stopped**!

Gerund (-*ing* form)

She **hates/doesn't mind being asked** questions.
Being photographed is a problem for some celebrities.

Infinitive

We **want to be given** more time. Don't **wait to be asked**.

Notes

The passive: present continuous, past continuous, and simple future

Form

- We form the present continuous and past continuous passive by using *am/is/are* or *was/were* + *being* + past participle.

  Active: *My mom **is feeding** my baby brother right now.*

  Passive: *My baby brother **is being fed** right now.*

  Active: *Angry workers **were attacking** the police.*

  Passive: *The police **were being attacked** by angry workers.*

- We form the simple future passive by using *will* + *be* + past participle.

  Active: *The teacher **will give** the students their grades tomorrow.*

  Passive: *The students **will be given** their grades tomorrow.*

The passive: modals, gerund (-*ing* form), and infinitive

Form

- We form modal passives by using a modal verb + *be* + past participle.

  Active: *You **must do** this project tonight.*

  Passive: *This project **must be done** tonight.*

- We form the passive of verbs which are followed by the gerund (-*ing* form) in active sentences by using verb + *being* + past participle.

  Active: *I love men **giving me** flowers.*

  Passive: *I love **being given** flowers.*

- We form the passive of verbs which are followed by the infinitive in active sentences by using verb + *to be* + past participle.

  Active: *I **have to tell** you twice before you do anything.*

  Passive: *You **have to be told** twice before you do anything.*

Grammar Practice

The passive: simple present, simple past, present perfect, past perfect

1 ★★ **Complete the sentences with the correct form of the verb *to be*.**

1 I *'ve* just ___*been*___ given a new phone.

2 My baby sister _____ always fed at 6:00.

3 Have you seen the news today? The local police station _____ just _____ robbed!

4 We _____ already _____ given Math, English, and Science homework today.

5 Yesterday, we _____ told to arrive at 9:00 so why is the building locked?

6 All the newspaper articles _____ read every afternoon by the editors.

7 A boy from our school _____ arrested yesterday.

2 ★★ **Complete the second sentence in the passive so that it means the same as the original sentence.**

1 People eat pizzas all over the world.

Pizzas _____*are eaten*_____ all over the world.

2 Our teacher didn't tell us about the English test!
We _____
about the English test.

3 When I arrived at my new school, two girls showed me to my classroom.
When I arrived at my new school, I _____
_____ to my classroom by two girls.

4 The students at this school write all the articles in the school newsletter.
All the articles in the school newsletter _____
_____ by students at this school.

5 You've copied this homework from the Internet!
This homework _____
from the Internet.

The passive: present continuous, past continuous, and simple future

3 ★★ **Where are the celebrities? Use the cues to write present continuous passive sentences.**

1 The Buckhams / introduce / to fans in Milan
The Buckhams are being introduced to fans in Milan.

2 Kid Jason / drive / the airport / to fly home / to the U.S.
_____
_____

3 Mad Donna / photograph / for a fashion magazine
_____
_____

4 Johnny Dipper / question / police
_____
_____

5 Take This / film / in concert
_____
_____

4 ★★ It is now 2 P.M. Look at the information and write sentences in the past continuous or simple future passive form.

1 10 A.M. this morning: fans / ask for autographs
This morning the Buckhams *were being asked for autographs* by fans.

2 8 P.M. tonight: Kid Jason's manager / meet him at the airport
Tonight Kid Jason _____ _____ by his manager.

3 10 A.M. this morning: fans / chase / Take This
This morning Take This _____ _____ by their fans.

4 8 P.M. tonight: the police / allow Johnny Dipper / to go home
Johnny Dipper _____ _____ to go home tonight.

5 10 A.M. this morning: trainer / give Mad Donna / a massage
This morning Mad Donna _____ _____ by her trainer.

The passive: modals, gerund (-*ing* form), and infinitive

5 ★★ Complete the sentences using the correct passive form.

Rules for reporters and photographers working here

1 You can't take photos of celebrities without asking them first.
Photos *can't be taken* of celebrities without asking them first.

2 You should always tell the truth.
The truth _____.

3 You can't photograph the children of celebrities.
The children of celebrities _____.

4 You shouldn't chase celebrities at high speed.
Celebrities _____ at high speed.

5 If you want to be a good tabloid reporter you must forget all these rules.
All these rules _____ if you want to be a good tabloid reporter!

6 ★★ Circle the correct answers. Then complete the sentences with the infinitive or gerund (-*ing* form) of the verbs in parentheses.

1 A good worker *needs* / *doesn't need* to be shown (show) what to do.

2 A polite guest *waits* / *doesn't wait* _____ (ask) to sit down.

3 A good student *has* / *doesn't have* _____ (help) with his or her homework.

4 A lazy person *likes* / *doesn't like* _____ (give) a lot of homework.

5 A shy person *loves* / *hates* _____ (invite) to parties.

Consolidation

7 Complete the story with the correct form of the verbs from the box.

• arrest • ask • drive • follow • keep • put
• photograph • question • stop • take • tell

The two movie stars, Jack Star and Pamela Lush, sat unhappily in the cold police station. They ¹*had been arrested* two hours earlier when they ² _____ by police for driving too fast. When they ³ _____ why they had been driving so fast, they explained that they had been trying to escape from paparazzi. Now, they ⁴ _____ by one of the police officers again.
"Can you tell us why you were driving so fast?" asked the police officer.
"I told you. We ⁵ _____ by photographers," answered Jack. "We didn't want ⁶ _____ together. We ⁷ _____ by the head of the movie studio that our relationship should ⁸ _____ secret."
"Don't worry," said the policeman, "we won't tell anyone." He picked up a telephone and, a few minutes later, said, "A car is coming for you in about thirty minutes."
Jack and Pamela ⁹ _____ to a small room where they waited for the car.

The happy ending
Jack and Pamela ¹⁰ _____ to the studio and their relationship stayed a secret.

The unhappy ending
A reporter was arrested and ¹¹ _____ into the same room as them . . .

Conditional: *if* clause + past perfect

Affirmative

If I/you/he/she/it/we/they **had arrived** earlier, I **would have made** you dinner.

I/You/He/She/It/We/They **would have waited if** you **had called** us.

Negative

I/You/He/She/It/We/They **would have been** on time **if I hadn't gotten** lost.

If I/you/he/she/it/we/they **had been** quieter, they **wouldn't have heard** us.

Questions and short answers

Would she **have asked** you **if** she **had known** the answer?

Yes, she **would have**.

No, she **wouldn't have**.

wish/if only + past perfect

Affirmative

I wish/If only I **had done** more work.

I wish/If only they **had called** us.

Negative

I wish/If only we **hadn't forgotten** the food.

I wish/If only I **hadn't missed** the last train.

Conditional: *if* clause + *might have*

Affirmative

If I/you/he/she/it/we/they **had learned** French, I/you/he/she/it/we/they **might have moved** to France.

If I/you/he/she/it/we/they **had asked** someone for help, I/you/he/she/it/we/they **might have arrived** earlier.

Negative

I/You/He/She/It/We/They **might have figured out** the answer together **if** I/you/he/she/it/we/they **hadn't had** an argument.

I/You/He/She/It/We/They **might not have missed** the plane **if** I/you/he/she/it/we/they **hadn't stopped** to buy a drink.

Notes

Conditional + past perfect

Usage

- We use the conditional + past perfect to imagine what would have happened if we had done something differently in the past.

Form

- We form the conditional + past perfect using two clauses: *If* + past perfect and *would* + *have* + past participle. We separate the two clauses with a comma.
  *If you **had told** the truth, you **wouldn't have gotten** into trouble.*

- We can write the two clauses in reverse order without a comma.
  *You **wouldn't have gotten** into trouble **if** you **had told** the truth.*

- We can replace *would* with *might* when we don't know exactly what would have happened if the past was changed.
  *If it **had rained** yesterday, I **wouldn't have gone** out.* (Definitely.)
  *If it **had rained** yesterday, I **might have watched** TV or I **might have read** a book.* (I don't know for sure.)

Common mistakes

If I didn't go to school, I would have been in trouble. ✗
If I hadn't gone to school, I would have been in trouble. ✓
If you hadn't asked me to the party, I might not have went. ✗
If you hadn't asked me to the party, I might not have gone. ✓

wish/if only + past perfect

Usage

- We use *wish/if only* + past perfect to show that we regret something that happened or didn't happen in the past and would have liked it to have been different.

Common mistakes

If only I didn't go to bed late last night. ✗
If only I hadn't gone to bed late last night. ✓
I wish we had a video camera yesterday. ✗
I wish we had had a video camera yesterday. ✓

Conditional: *if* clause + past perfect

1 ★ **Complete the conditional sentences with the correct form of the verbs in parentheses.**

1 If I ___had gone___ (go) out last night, I *wouldn't have finished* (not finish) my homework.

2 If Tom _____ (not be) with me, I _____ (not know) anyone there.

3 If Carole _____ (not find) the key, we _____ (not be able) to get in the house.

4 David and Victoria _____ (stay) longer if the paparazzi _____ (not try) to take photographs of their children.

5 If my teachers _____ (point out) my mistakes during the year, I _____ (not have) so many problems in my exams.

6 My friend's uncle _____ (give) me a lot of money for my old toys if you _____ (not give) them away.

7 If my dad _____ (drive) more carefully, he _____ (not have) an accident.

8 We _____ (get) wet if we _____ (go) camping last week.

2 ★★ **Complete the sentences so that they mean the same as the originals. Use the correct form of the words in parentheses.**

The party

1 If Mark had stayed longer, he would have had a good time. (not leave so early)
Mark *would have had a good time if he hadn't left so early* .

2 If you hadn't invited so many people, there would have been enough food. (invite fewer)
There _____
_____ .

3 If you'd told me I should look nice, I'd have worn a dress. (not wear jeans)
I _____
_____ .

The reporters

4 The paparazzi followed the celebrity because he was with a new girlfriend. (not be/not follow)
If _____
_____ .

5 If you hadn't left out the information about the Oscars, that would have been an excellent article. (remember)
That _____
_____ .

The police

6 The police arrested the group of teenagers because they vandalized the bus stop. (not vandalize/not arrest)
If they _____
_____ .

7 You were stopped by the police because they thought you were a burglar. (not think/not stop)
If _____
_____ .

wish/if only + past perfect

3 ★ **Write the words in the correct order.**

1 I / been / friend / wish / hadn't / my / to / rude / I
I wish I hadn't been rude to my friend.

2 had / we / If / the / time / on / left / only / house

_____

3 eat / If / out / decided / we / only / to / had

_____

4 hadn't / here / wish / I / party / a / had / I

_____

5 driven / carefully / more / wish / I / I / had

_____

6 only / brought / I / If / other / my / camera / had

_____

4 ★★ Rewrite the regrets using *if only* or *I wish*, then match them to the people in Exercise 3.

1 Why didn't we get here earlier?

If only *we had gotten here earlier. Person 2*

2 Why didn't I check the batteries?

I wish _____

3 Why did I promise to cook dinner?

I wish _____

4 Why did I invite so many people?

If only _____

5 Why did I drive so fast?

I wish _____

6 Why did I say those things to her?

If only _____

Conditional: *if* clause + *might have*

5 ★★ Write sentences using the cues.

1 you / not invite / me to your party → might go / to the theater

If you hadn't invited me to your party, I might
have gone to the theater.

2 we / not win / that money → might not have / a vacation last year

_____

_____

3 you / spend / more time doing your homework → might be / better

_____

_____

4 my phone / not ring → might not wake up

_____

_____

5 police / arrive / sooner → might catch / the burglar

_____

_____

6 you / not wear / jeans to the interview → might get / the job

_____

_____

6 ★★ Write sentences about how things could have been different.

> I broke my arm when I was fifteen and I couldn't exercise any more. I decided to join the theater club and, very soon, I got a part in the school play. The local newspaper wrote about it and a local theater group heard about me. They asked me to join. That's when I started to take acting seriously. Soon afterwards, I moved to New York where I lived for three years. I appeared on TV a few times and finally, two years ago, I moved to Hollywood.

✓ = would have	✗ = wouldn't have
? = might have	?✗ = might not have

1 not break arm → ✓ exercise

If I hadn't broken my arm, I would have exercised.

2 exercised → ?✗ go to the theater club

If I had exercised, I might not have joined the theater club.

3 not join the theater club → ✗ get part in the school play

_____

_____

4 not get part in the school play → ✗ the local newspaper write about me

_____

_____

5 local paper not write about the show → ?✗ the local theater group hear about me

_____

_____

6 not take acting seriously → ?✗ move to New York

_____

_____

7 not live in New York → ? study at college

_____

_____

Consolidation

7 Six of the sentences are incorrect. Find five more incorrect sentences and rewrite them correctly.

> I loved Take That when I was younger.

had stayed

1 I wish they ~~stayed~~ together. ✗
                ∧

2 If Robbie Williams hadn't been so successful, he might have joined them again. ✓

3 If only I saw them in concert. ☐

> I love playing my *Sims 2* video games.

4 If Will Wright didn't meet Jeff Braun, they wouldn't have started the company Maxis Software. ☐

5 Will might not have the idea for *The Sims* games if his house hadn't burned down. ☐

6 I wish my brother didn't sell all his old *SimCity* video games. ☐

7 If only George brought a map on his hiking trip. ☐

8 If he had planned his trip better, he would have brought a map and a compass. ☐